Indigenous
Voices

Indigenous
Voices

Inspiring & Empowering Quotes from Global Thought Leaders

TATÉ WALKER

wellfleet
press

ARTIST Steve Smith (Dla'kwagila), Eagle Chilkat, Oweekeno, Kwakwaka'wakw

Contents

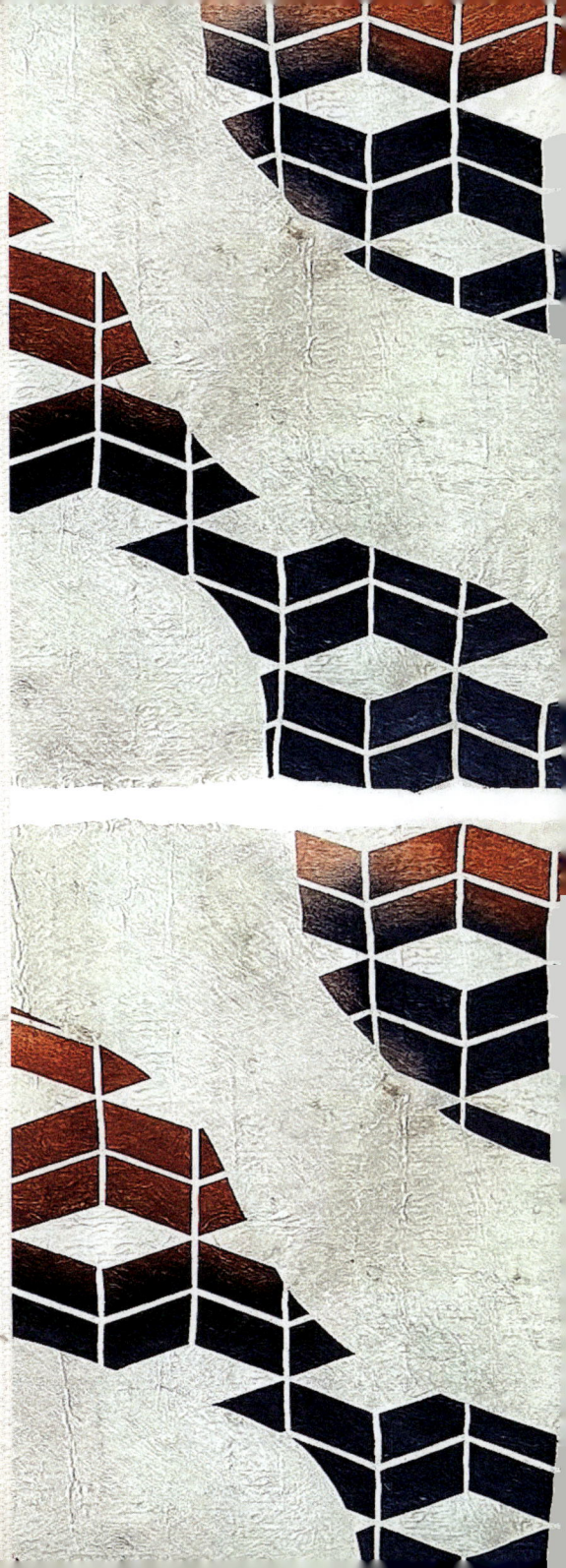

ARTIST Lehuauakea, *Kānehunamoku*, Native Hawaiian

Introduction

The late Sicangu Lakota language teacher and preservationist Albert White Hat, Sr., once said, "Language is culture is language." Seen by many as an expert for his role in developing Lakota-English dictionaries, creating pronunciation and conversation videos, and developing other vital teaching strategies, White Hat explained that without language, there is no culture or spirituality, or at least no real understanding of those ways of being. For Lakota people like me, language is a relative, a living entity that needs breath and blood and desire to exist.

Estimates suggest fewer than sixteen thousand people speak one of the languages of the Oceti Sakowin (a confederacy of Lakota, Dakota, and Nakota nations who speak a similar language with dialect variations) at home. Fluency has much lower numbers. Few Indigenous peoples of my mother's generation and younger grew up with a traditional language as our first tongue. There are several reasons why. For example, as a news journalist who has covered Indigenous issues since the early 2000s, I have listened to too many elders tell harrowing stories of the abuse they suffered in residential schools, often for speaking their tribal language. This is just one reason why many chose not to teach their children or grandchildren the language.

Still, pieces of our language survived, and like any relative, Lakotiyapi—the Lakota language—has grown with intentional use and care. While I would test at a toddler level in terms of retention and understanding of the language, I am one of many millennials using social media, old texts, and audio recordings to slowly learn Lakotiyapi, thanks to the efforts of people like White Hat and Eugene "Ray" Taken Alive, who is the first person quoted in the first chapter of this book for the work he does to ensure the Lakota language stays free, accessible, and relevant to Lakota people.

ARTIST Hattie Lee Mendoza, *Having Company*, Cherokee

Written and verbal language fluency is just one aspect of communication, and the Lakota, like Indigenous peoples across the globe, are continuing language legacies through written orthographies, yes, but also through entertainment, medicine, food, body work, policy, and many other mediums through which relationships are developed and strengthened. This book highlights those good relatives on the front pages and front lines of their regions' most vital issues.

The everyday warriors of the Great Plains continue to fight on multiple fronts to protect their lands and waters, their images, and their languages, as exemplified by Taken Alive. The nations of the Pacific Northwest remain strongly tied to the stories of trees, rivers, and fish because of the psychologists, gardeners, journalists, and fire keepers translating those histories through their work. The experiences endured by the people of the Eastern Woodlands are rooted in their relationships with food sovereignty, queerness, Afro-Indigenous love, and language immersion at the earliest ages.

The influential leaders representing the South/Southeast region of the United States and the Caribbean are extraordinary innovators in their respective fields of app development, spacecraft, and fiction writing. In the Southwest, voices from the desert are anything but dry and barren; instead, their hearts fuel decades of work to archive ancestral memory, build sustainable communities, and empower imaginations. The people representing California's tribal nations are as diverse as the beautiful landscapes across the state, but each voice is a leader moving its community through the work of rematriation, reparations, reconnecting, tribal communications, and scholarship, with an eye toward the next generations. This book closes on those nations of Indigenous peoples unconfined and undefined by colonial borders in Alaska, Hawai'i, Mexico, and Canada.

Basic cultural competence is one of the biggest challenges Indigenous peoples face. Our works depend on establishing context, translating concepts, and getting our audiences up to speed in order to facilitate more informed conversations.

Most of us never give the 202-level presentation because no one has passed the intro course. Let's review: Christopher Columbus did not discover what we now call the United States. It is a continuous effort (and often exhausting) to remind people that we don't speak for all tribal people, that there are hundreds and thousands of sovereign tribal nations across the globe, and that the fight against colonial systems begins with recognizing whose land you're on. But it is necessary.

As this book breathes each voice onto the page, remember: Indigenous peoples are not a monolith. Left unchecked, mainstream media/society lumps Indigenous histories and modern-day experiences together. Homogenization perpetuates the harm and disparities Indigenous peoples face. It is important not to do that here. Being "Indigenous" is so much more than a racial category, although colonial institutions, such as the United States Census Bureau, classify it as such.

More accurately, to be Indigenous is to be a political entity with a sovereign connection to place and nation that predates colonial rule. For instance, each of the 574 federally recognized tribes in the United States—a number that can change on the whim of the current administration—have a unique nation-to-nation relationship with the United States government, which has a trust responsibility to protect and support tribal nations through treaties, statutes, and other legal agreements. These tribal nations have the right to self-governance, including establishing their own systems of education, business, health, policing, and citizenship. Dig deeper: These 574 nations have their own languages, spirituality practices, relationship dynamics, and other nation-specific beliefs and behaviors. There are hundreds of other tribes in the United States that aren't federally recognized—of course, they are sovereign nations at their core, but they have no federal protections or rights to land, healthcare, or other supports the United States government agreed to via treaties in exchange for the lands it occupies today.

The undeniably political and elemental nature of what it means to be *of*—
not from—somewhere is why this book showcases living Indigenous voices
intentionally grouped by place. When a lawyer or shoemaker of the Great Plains
is described as an "everyday hero," it's not that voices of other regions aren't
also heroic or the shoemaker couldn't also be described as an "innovator," like
the peoples of the South/Southeastern region. Instead, imagine the voices of
this book like the stars of a night sky; the themes are the constellations.

Together, the voices in each theme are telling a story of their region: The Great
Plains voices protecting their lands, languages, and images represent Everyday
Warriors to flip the narrative of the wild savage. The potlatch, once outlawed,
is a ceremony practiced widely among tribes of the Pacific Northwest, and it
exemplifies the power of the region's Stories and Tellers who forage, fish, and
otherwise keep traditions alive in the face of genocide. The Eastern Woodlands
has a history many associate with devastating disease and thanksgiving
massacres, but the voices of chiefs, actors, and authors prioritize their Roots
and Relations grounded in family and passion.

From billion-dollar casino deals with groundbreaking sports betting apps to
geoscientists writing bestselling YA fiction, the Innovators and Influencers
representing the South/Southeast region of the United States and the
Caribbean are anything but stuck in the past. In the Southwest, building
sustainable communities, imagining poetic futures, and redefining politics is
the definition of Desert Heartwork. California has seen its share of disasters,
none so ruinous as missionaries—play Seven Degrees of Climate Change and it
all comes back to colonizers. Rebuilding is hard, but Reconnecting the Sacred
is what the voices of tribes across the state are accomplishing in big and small
ways, from coming-of-age ceremonies to meeting long-lost family members.
The crescendo rises from Indigenous folks living Beyond Borders, literally and
figuratively. These voices are unconfined by societal expectations, be they from
a traditional tattoo artist, abortion rights activist, or a spiritual medium.

This book features contemporary voices, which is crucial on so many levels. If you do an internet search for "Native American quotes," you'll find a smorgasbord of headdresses and warpaint next to immaculate proverbs. So much is lost, edited, or embellished in translation. Rather than showcase text that's rolled out every November with unverifiable translations or context, this book honors oral storytelling traditions and allows readers to enjoy snapshots of contemporary conversations; about seventy-five percent of the voices featured in this book were curated via one-on-one phone, internet, or in-person interviews. This book is a celebration of voices doing good work and building community today. The voices reverberating throughout ring with authenticity, relatability, and logic.

Indigenous Voices honors the vastness of identities included under the umbrellas of American Indians (a legal term for tribal peoples of the United States, also Native Americans, Natives, or Indians, when referenced within community), Indigenous peoples of Canada (including First Nations, Metis, and Inuit), Native Hawaiians and other Pacific Islanders, Alaska Natives, and the many tribal peoples of Mexico. Moreover, Indigenous—a capital "I" when referring to people or our products—often refers to any original peoples actively resisting imperialism, such as those in Polynesia, Central and South America, Palestine, Sudan, and Congo. This is why the enormity of lands, languages, cultures, and ideas embedded within a word like Indigenous defies easy or neat description. To be Indigenous is to carry the trauma of genocide and settler colonialism across generations of survivors. It is also an understanding that there is more to Indigeneity than disparity, oppression, and resilience; there are rich histories, rematriation, reclamation, radical joy, and radiant futures. The voices of this book balance all of this and more in ways that uplift kin and community.

Everyday Warriors

◀◆▶

Everyday Warriors know their accomplishments aren't solo acts meant for recognition, medals, or glory. Battles won in courtrooms, classrooms, camps along riverbanks, movie theaters, and fashion runways are fought with knowledge passed down by the ancestors and inspired by the next generations.

Paired with the Great Plains, the word warrior will often conjure the stereotypes that plague and homogenize all Indigenous peoples—think tipis, peace pipes, and headdresses. The association harkens back to the Wild West, when land and lawlessness lured politicians and fortune-seekers westward despite legal treaties in place to prevent such things. The tribes that refused settler colonialism were depicted as bloodthirsty savages and threats to civilization. To a growing society trying to manifest its destiny, "Indigenous" and "warrior" evoked unfavorable connotations. In Lakotiyapi, *akicita* is often translated as "warrior," although "guardian" is more accurate. While *akicita* did/do battle, they exist to protect the *oyate*, the people, an earned privilege with tremendous responsibility. Alongside their warriors, tribal nations flourished pre-contact across the Great Plains, which is physiographically defined by a massive slice of prairie, grasslands, and mountainous formations across the central United States, extending north into Canada, south through Texas, east to the Mississippi River, and west to the Rocky Mountains.

More than thirty nations are historically and/or legally considered to be of the Great Plains region. The following sequence shares regional voices making warrior-like efforts to continue their ancestral legacies while also honoring community practices within mainstream institutions. There's the artist who is a ribbon-winning expert at creating armor-like adornments because beadwork—and the mental focus it demands—is a safe place for him to escape. And there's basketball, which for two voices is the magic way they connect with and inspire Native youth. There are lawyers, linguists, and elders—all guardians of their lands, peoples, and cultures.

Stories that have been told for countless generations, words and phrases that have been said for countless generations, language that has been said for countless generations, songs that have been sung for countless generations are now being packaged, locked away, and sold. Whether we're aware of it or not, it's happening. The very people the language belongs to are being forced to buy it back or just sit on our hands with our mouths shut while others profit, manipulate, and abuse our words, songs, and stories. Our language belongs to our children and the next generations. It's our responsibility now to fight, to hold onto what's ours, and to reclaim what has been taken. Colonization and greed are always lurking, and so we must always be vigilant.

EUGENE "RAY" TAKEN ALIVE
Hunkpapa Lakota, Lakota Language Teacher

EUGENE "RAY" TAKEN ALIVE (B. 1987, HE/HIM) is Hunkpapa Lakota and a citizen of the Standing Rock Sioux Tribe. He is an educator and credited as a Lakota dub executive producer for Marvel Studios' *The Avengers* (2024). He went viral on social media in the 2010s for his short, funny videos that ended with "Don't you know I'm on council!?" Things became serious when Taken Alive tried to use the language materials his late grandmother had created in collaboration with a nonprofit led by two white European men. Since his grandmother's death, Taken Alive and his family have worked to reclaim all rights to her Lakota language materials from the nonprofit, which accused him of copyright infringement, threatened to sue him, and unsuccessfully sought to strip Taken Alive and his wife of their teaching licenses. Taken Alive is at the forefront of a growing movement working to ensure all recordings, curriculum, textbooks, dictionaries, and other products created to teach tribal languages are free and accessible to the originating Indigenous communities.

When I first started learning the Ojibwe Language, every elder I asked for help told me the same thing: "If you want to really know the culture, history, philosophy, and spirituality of the people, it is all in the Language." It's remarkable to consider that every time we use the Ojibwe Language, we are enjoying an investment in us that is thousands of years old. We must continue to teach and pass on the Ojibwe Language so that those seven generations from now can also come to understand and live mino-bimaadiziwin "the good life."

JAMES VUKELICH KAAGEGAABAW
Ojibwe, Ojibwe Language Teacher and Author

JAMES VUKELICH KAAGEGAABAW (B. 1975, HE/HIM), a descendant of Turtle Mountain, is a renowned international speaker, author, and digital creator. He is known on social media for his series of short videos on Indigenous language and culture. He is the author of *The Seven Generations and the Seven Grandfather Teachings* and the children's book, *Wisdom Weavers,* which introduces the Ojibwe language to young audiences. His keen insights were developed through speaking with and recording elders and Native language speakers across North America as part of the *Ojibwe Language Dictionary Project*. Kaagegaabaw is a passionate advocate for sharing how to live a life of *mino-bimaadiziwin*—the good life. For over twenty years, he has facilitated community language tables, worked as an educator from pre-k to university levels, consulted with public and private organizations on language and cultural programs, and traveled internationally as a keynote speaker. He has been featured in numerous publications, podcasts, and radio and television programs. Kaagegaabaw lives in the Twin Cities, Minnesota, with his wife and son.

> Beadwork has saved my life so many times. Beadwork was and still is my escape from the world. I don't think I would still be here if I didn't do beadwork. I've been in some very traumatic situations during my lifetime, but beadwork saw me through it all. Beading is very therapeutic and helps me stay calm and process everything.

ELIAS JADE NOT AFRAID
Apsáalooke, Beadworker and Designer

◄◆►

ELIAS JADE NOT AFRAID (B. 1990, HE/HIM) is a member of the Apsáalooke Nation and grew up on the Crow Reservation in Montana. He is a world-renowned, genre-defying artist with awards and ribbons for media spanning from beadwork to fashion, from makeup to textiles. As a self-taught artist who grew up surrounded by his grandmother's traditional Apsáalooke art and research, Not Afraid is known for creating high-fashion wearable art made to survive everyday use through the generations, as well as for sharing art tips and techniques freely on social media. He is also celebrated for developing unique and innovative pieces for runways, red carpets, brand names, and museums. Not Afraid's work has been sold at Nordstrom, has adorned celebrities in magazines, and is a permanent fixture in the New York Metropolitan Museum of Art, the Field Museum, the Minneapolis Institute of Art, and the Smithsonian, among others.

ARTIST Elias Jade Not Afraid, *Geometric Florals*

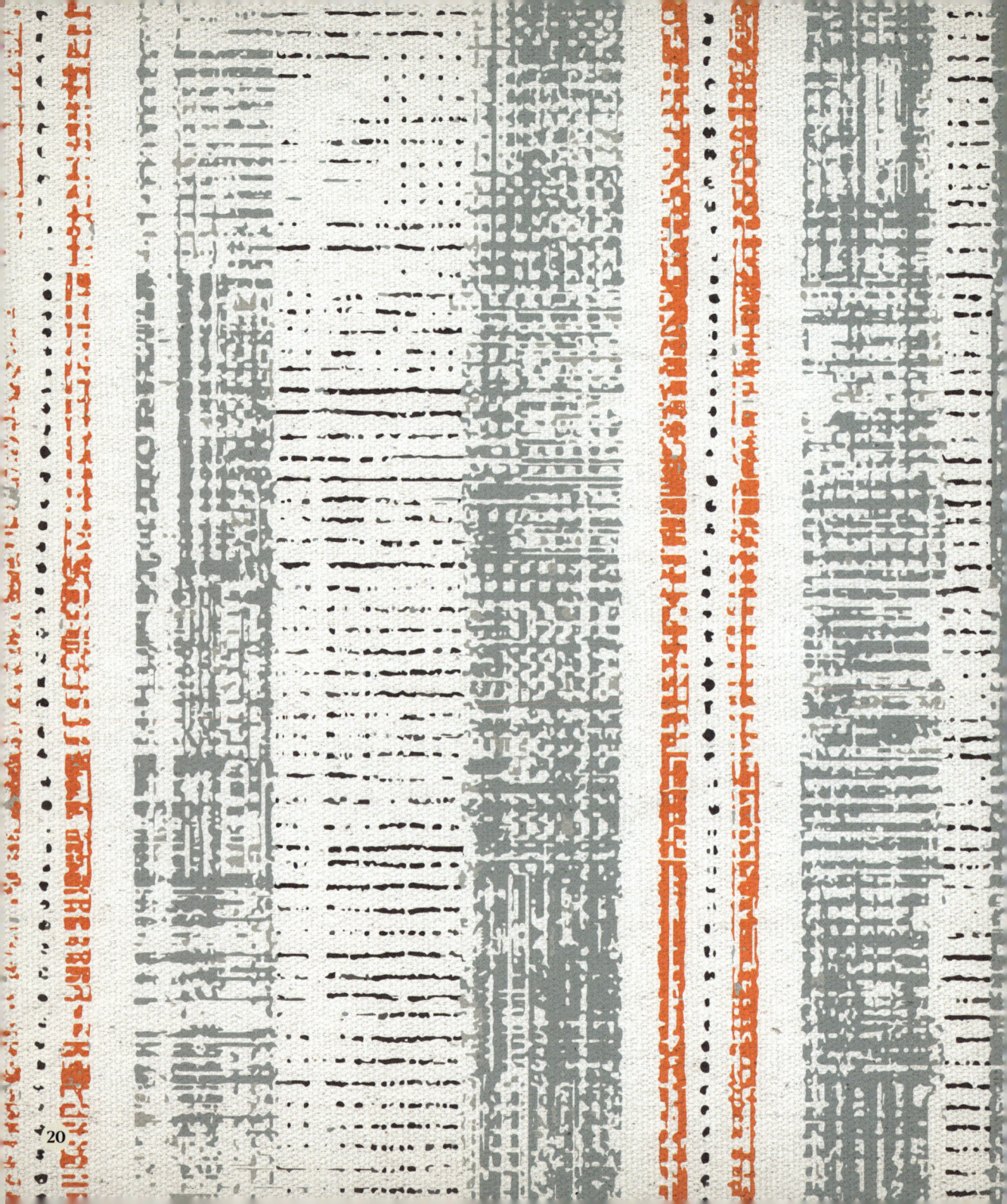

My grandma would always talk to me about sharing my medicine. She said my medicine was laughter, because I could make anyone laugh. I think that's always, in a way, what I've tried to do, even in racing—bring joy to others and myself. It's important to find something you love to do that gives you a sense of peace while challenging you to be the best person you can be. That's your medicine.

CHERI BECERRA MADSEN
Omaha, Paralympian

CHERI BECERRA MADSEN (B. 1976, SHE/HER) is a member of the Omaha Tribe of Nebraska. She was three when she lost the use of her legs, but that didn't keep her from accomplishing her dream of racing. She is a track and field Paralympic medalist and wheelchair racing athlete who was the first Native American female to win an Olympic exhibition bronze medal (800m), which she earned at the 1996 Olympics in Atlanta. She stopped racing in 2001 to start a family. She had no intentions of racing again, but after her father and brother died in a car accident in 2007, she decided to return to racing to honor her brother, who she learned dreamed of seeing his nieces watch their mother on the Olympic podium. She won silver (400m) at Rio de Janeiro in 2016, and silver (400m) and bronze (100m) at Tokyo in 2020. At several points in her three-decade-long career, Becerra Madsen held the world record in the 100m, 200m, and 400m wheelchair racing events and won several national and international championships. Becerra Madsen retired from racing in 2024.

JOHN ECHOHAWK (B. 1945, HE/HIM) is a member of the Pawnee Nation and is the co-founder and executive director of the Native American Rights Fund (NARF), which has been pivotal in protecting and furthering tribal sovereignty and the civil rights of Native people in the United States since its inception in 1970. Echohawk was the first graduate of the University of New Mexico's special program to train Indian lawyers, and he was a founding member of the American Indian Law Students Association while in law school. He was recognized as one of the one hundred most influential lawyers in America by the National Law Journal, and Echohawk was honored with the American Bar Association's prestigious Thurgood Marshall Award in 2023. With little hesitation, however, Echohawk said he's most proud of NARF's role in filing an amicus curiae brief in the 1987 United States Supreme Court case *California v. the Cabazon Band of Mission Indians*, which upheld the sovereign right of Native nations to operate gaming businesses and generate gambling revenue on their own lands, one of the biggest economic drivers in Indian Country.

My message to younger generations of Native people is [that] they all need to come to appreciate their citizenship in their tribe and recognize it's a sovereign nation. That sovereignty is always being challenged. Every generation has to step up and meet those challenges. I want everybody to understand their role as citizens of sovereign Indian nations is first to help protect that sovereignty and second to help educate people about that sovereignty. That's the biggest problem we have, and one we keep working on here at the Native American Rights Fund, is educating non–Natives about Indian sovereignty. Most Americans don't know about it—or much about it—due to major gaps in our education systems with teaching Native American issues and accurate history.

JOHN ECHOHAWK
Pawnee, Co-Founder/Executive Director of the Native American Rights Fund

The Ioway people, we believe everything has life in it, and that means there is still life in the ancestral remains left in those boxes down in museum or university storage or being held in a private collection somewhere. We just want those ancestors to go back on their journeys. If you have our ancestors displayed, or in a box somewhere—whether you're a big organization or a small collector—you're preventing that from happening. When we return the ancestors and help them back on their journeys, we also help the world go back into balance. And we believe that's why the world is out of balance and has been out of balance for a long time.

LANCE M. FOSTER
Ioway, Elder, Author, and Historian

LANCE M. FOSTER (B. 1960, HE/HIM) is Ioway and a member of the Iowa Tribe of Kansas and Nebraska. He serves as a tribal historic preservation officer for his tribe and consults on environmental and cultural compliance. Foster founded the Iowa Tribal Museum and Cultural Center, is an Ioway language advocate, and is an enforcement officer for the Native American Graves Protection and Repatriation Act. In 2019, Foster was elected tribal vice chairman. He also led successful efforts to establish Ioway Tribal National Park (Baxoje Mowotanani) and reclaimed the tribal boarding school (Presbyterian Mission) for the Ioway people. He is the author of *The Indians of Iowa* (2009). Foster earned a bachelor's degree in anthropology and Native American studies from the University of Montana, and master's degrees in anthropology and landscape architecture from Iowa State University. He is also an alumnus of the Institute of American Indian Arts. He was the director of the Native Rights, Land, and Culture Division of the Office of Hawaiian Affairs, a historical landscape architect for the National Park Service, and an archaeologist for the United States Forest Service.

There [are] more important things in life than what we see on TV. There's family, there's tradition, there's culture. The materialistic things come and go. You can never control those things. But the thing you can control is how good of a person you are. I think being around my family and relatives and tribes and trying to give back to my community, I think that's shaped me into the person I am today, and that just translates to the basketball court.

LINDY WATERS III
Kiowa, Cherokee, NBA Player

LINDY WATERS III (B. 1997, HE/HIM) is a citizen of the Kiowa Tribe of Oklahoma and the Cherokee Nation. He is an NBA player for the Golden State Warriors as of June 2024, and he played for the Oklahoma City Thunder from 2022 to 2024. Waters received a bachelor of science in 2020 from Oklahoma State University; he finished his college basketball career with over 1,000 points, 250 assists, and 100 steals. Waters was named "Indian of the Year" in 2018 by the American Indian Exposition, one of the nation's oldest and largest intertribal celebrations. In 2022, he founded the Lindy Waters III Foundation, which enhances and supports Native American youth and Indigenous communities through sports, health and wellness, and leadership programs. For this work, Waters was a finalist for the 2023 to 2024 Kareem Abdul-Jabbar Social Justice Champion Award, an annual honor for an NBA player making strides in the fight for social justice. In 2024, Waters was also inducted into the North American Indigenous Athletics Hall of Fame.

If you're depending on an entity to give you money or solutions—and that entity resents your existence—then the only solutions you're going to get are abject poverty and despair. So, I've tried really hard to ensure that we're over here baking a bigger cake, rather than fighting over someone else's crumbs . . . Everybody wants to have a better life. The system makes it hard for tribes to be successful, so I've decided to co-opt that system to be as successful as possible and share that success with as many people as possible.

LANCE MORGAN
Ho-Chunk, President and CEO of Ho-Chunk, Inc.

LANCE MORGAN (B. 1969, HE/HIM) is Ho-Chunk and a member of the Winnebago Tribe of Nebraska. Morgan is the president and CEO of Ho-Chunk, Inc., which he launched in 1994 with a twenty-five-thousand-dollar investment from his tribe and one employee. In 2022, Ho-Chunk, Inc. reported annual revenues of approximately $380 million and more than two thousand employees. Ho-Chunk, Inc. has been nationally recognized with the Innovations in Government Award (sponsored by Harvard University and the Ford Foundation), the Minority Business Magazine's Entrepreneurial Spirit Award, the United States Department of State and Department of Commerce, and others. Morgan was named a Champion of Change by the White House in 2011; he was presented the Nebraska Builder Award by the University of Nebraska in 2012; and he was appointed to the Board of Trustees of the Smithsonian's National Museum of American Indian in 2013 and 2014. Morgan earned a bachelor's degree in economics from the University of Nebraska in 1990, and his juris doctorate from Harvard Law School in 1993. He is a member of the Minnesota Bar Association and the Winnebago Tribal Court.

My work is deeply rooted in the observation of Northern Cheyenne beadwork and quillwork. There is a desire for connection I am celebrating through all the digital elements and symmetrical elements. My mom was adopted in the 1960s, so in studying this work, I sometimes feel like an outsider. I did not grow up with family who could teach me to bead, so these perfect replications of symbols repeated over and over is like my own way to respect these ancestors and their original artwork. As somebody who paints objects of permanence, I hope one day, when I'm an ancestor, people will admire my dedication to craft, yes, but more importantly, remember me as a good human who contributed love—to family, to peers, to society.

JORDAN ANN CRAIG
Northern Cheyenne, Painter, Printmaker, Designer, Photographer, and Business Entrepreneur

JORDAN ANN CRAIG (B. 1992, SHE/HER), a member of the Northern Cheyenne Tribe of Montana and of Zuni descent, is an award-winning painter, printmaker, designer, photographer, and entrepreneur. Craig's work has been shown across the globe in galleries, on runways, in magazines, and in collaborations with brands like Merrell and Rumpl. She received a bachelor's degree from Dartmouth College and was awarded the H. Allen Brooks Traveling Fellowship in 2017 as well as the Eric and Barbara Dobkin Fellowship at the School for Advanced Research. In 2019, Craig and her sister Madison founded the apparel brand Shy Natives, known for its handmade gender expansive lingerie and ethically sourced materials. Since 2023, she has served as a commissioner for the United States Department of the Interior's Indian Arts and Crafts Board. In 2024, Craig and her mother, Brigit Johnson, received funding from Creative Capital for Books Not Returned Library, a project raising awareness about Missing and Murdered Indigenous Women.

ARTIST Jordan Ann Craig, *Confessions of a Fairy Goddess*

Our cultures are living and breathing and thriving and constantly developing. That's why I create this clothing. I want to make accessible, affordable art that connects people to the designs and colors that they recognize as culturally theirs, that they can wear everyday with pride. A friend told me recently she saw someone wearing one of my dresses at a Sundance. To know that my work is worn in places of prayer, or at graduations, or birthday parties, or art markets, at work to look and feel good—that brings me so much joy. I'm connected to all these moments in a special way.

LAUREN GOOD DAY
Arikara, Hidatsa, Blackfeet, Plains Cree, Cultural Artist and Fashion Designer

LAUREN GOOD DAY (B. 1987, NONE) is an award-winning Arikara, Hidatsa, Blackfeet, and Plains Cree artist and fashion designer. Good Day is an enrolled member of the Three Affiliated Tribes (Mandan, Hidatsa, Arikara Nation) of the Ft. Berthold Reservation in North Dakota, and also a registered member of Sweetgrass First Nation in Treaty 6 Territory, Saskatchewan, Canada. Good Day is known for seamlessly combining Great Plains-style cultural art with modern aesthetics, and Good Day's work has been featured in the nation's most prestigious shows, museums, and publications, including the Santa Fe Indian Market, the Smithsonian's National Museum of the American Indian, *Vogue* magazine, and *The New York Times*. Good Day's work has adorned powwow royalty, Hollywood celebrities, and major brands. Promoting and revitalizing Indigenous arts with new methods and ideas is a passion for Good Day, who earned a bachelor's degree in art and Indigenous studies from the Institute of American Indian Arts.

SAM MCCRACKEN (B. 1960, HE/HIM) is Assiniboine and Sioux and a member of the Ft. Peck Tribes in Montana. McCracken is the general manager and visionary of Nike's N7 programs and founder of the N7 Fund, which has awarded more than $7.6 million in grants and has reached more than five hundred thousand youth since its inception in 2009. McCracken began his Nike tenure in 1997 at a warehouse. Nike asked him to manage the revitalization of their Native American Employee Network; shortly thereafter, McCracken proposed a business plan with the goal of increasing health and wellness through physical activity in Native communities. He was named manager of Nike's Native American Business in 2000, and he grew N7 into the inspirational brand it is today. McCracken has received numerous recognitions, including Sustainability.com's "20 Most Innovative Intrapreneurs" (2007), the National Indian Gaming Association President's Leadership Award (2010), and the National Center for American Indian Enterprise Development's Corporate Business of the Year award (2019). McCracken was appointed by President Barack Obama to the United States Department of Education's National Advisory Council on Indian Education.

N7 started as a vision of what I thought Nike could provide the Indigenous community. It was never about one individual. You come because you want to be part of it. I look back to learn and get guided instruction and focus from the generation before me, knowing that if I look up and look down the road there's someone behind me that's going to take these reins and make it bigger, better, and more powerful.

SAM MCCRACKEN
*Assiniboine, Sioux, General Manager of Nike N7
and Founder of Nike's N7 Fund*

Our basketball team was a beautiful distraction from the cold, dark winter months. Sometimes life on our reservation can be tough. But basketball has always been what brought us together, what made us all smile no matter what. I wrote *Rez Ball* with hope in my heart and as a love letter to all Indigenous communities where hoop dreams carry us above the rim and uplift us when we need it most.

BYRON GRAVES
Ojibwe, Author

◄◆►

BYRON GRAVES (B. 1982, HE/THEY) is an Ojibwe author who was born and raised on the Red Lake Indian Reservation in northern Minnesota. Their debut novel, *Rez Ball*, won the prestigious 2024 Walter C. Morris YA Debut Award, the 2024 American Indian Youth Literature Award, and the 2024 Colorado Book Award for Best Young Adult Novel. Graves also received 2024 honors from the Boston Globe–Horn Book Awards and the Whippoorwill Book Awards. The book follows Ojibwe teen Tre, who navigates life on the rez (reservation) while trying to balance friendships, romance, deep grief, and making the varsity basketball team. Graves draws on his own glory days of no-look passes, fadeaway jump shots, and a once-in-a-lifetime trip to the state tournament to give readers authentic characters and community. When Graves isn't writing, they're playing video games, skateboarding, or connecting with cats.

[T]hat one fleeting period in time was not what I took from the Olympics. What I took was the true sense of global unity through the dignity, the character, and beauty of global diversity. As an orphaned Indian boy, while living in the back seat of an old, wrecked car [for] several weeks, I dreamed of the Olympic Games. Being half Sioux Indian and half white . . . I felt I did not belong. The full-blood Indian called me mixed-blood; the white called me Indian. With both cultures rejecting me, I found a third culture called sport. The Olympic dream and the Olympic ideals became my culture . . . . Sport without value is meaningless. Sport used to teach life values is sacred.

BILLY MILLS
Oglala Lakota, Gold Medalist, 1964 Tokyo Olympics

BILLY MILLS (B. 1938, HE/HIM) is Oglala Lakota from the Pine Ridge Indian Reservation in South Dakota. His Lakota name is Tamakhóčhe Theȟíla (Respects the Earth). At the 1964 Olympics, Mills shocked the world when he unexpectedly pulled away from a deep field with just 100 meters to go to win gold in the longest track event at the games. At twenty-six, Mills set a then-world record for the 10,000-meter race at 28 minutes and 24.4 seconds. No United States athlete has achieved gold in the event since. At the time, Mills was a first lieutenant in the United States Marine Corps. When he returned from the Olympics, his tribe made him *akicita* (a community warrior). Mills attended the University of Kansas on a full scholarship, and he won consecutive NCAA All-American honors in cross country and graduated with a degree in education. In 1986, Mills co-founded Running Strong for American Indian Youth, an organization that supports cultural programs and provides health and housing assistance for Native American communities. Mills received the 2012 Presidential Citizens Medal from President Barack Obama.

Stories and Tellers

In the Pacific Northwest, fish, water, and tree relatives have shared space and stories since time immemorial. We learn through storytellers that salmon are sacred, part of many nations' creation histories and identities, dietary staples, and a form of currency. Today, tribes are using treaty language and the courts to fight for the rights of salmon to exist and flourish.

Vital waterways dammed with federal pen strokes in the mid-1900s to intentionally undermine and destroy the tribes who depended on them are slowly being returned to tribal control. Ancient trees once used to build massive canoes, monumental carvings, and woven practical and fine art are now being devastated by wildfires fueled by industrialization, consumer culture, and climate change. But a different tale could be told with the help of prescribed burns from those with knowledge of Indigenous fire medicine. These stories, those who tell them, and how those stories are told have incredible power. Connected to place, these stories and tellers are unstoppable.

The Pacific Northwest is a geographic region flanked by the Pacific Ocean and includes British Columbia, Washington State, Oregon, parts of northern California, and parts of Alaska. Western Montana and northern Idaho are often considered in this collective. This region was once one of the most densely populated areas for Native peoples. Left to mainstream media, the story of Pacific Northwest tribes would be clouded by twilight werewolves, anti-treaty propaganda, and disrespected totem poles. Voices of the Pacific Northwest are changing the narrative. There's the social psychologist doing groundbreaking research to push significant cultural change, like ending billion-dollar sports franchises' use of racist names and mascots. There's the professional fighter-turned football player-turned model who leaned into her family and culture to overcome intense trauma and now advocates for and inspires survivors of abuse. These and the other voices of this sequence are doing important work to accurately translate the region's stories of subsistence lifestyles, performance, fire medicine, and more.

ARTIST Steve Smith (Dla'kwagila), Eagle Chilkat, Oweekeno, Kwakwaka'wakw

*The willow tree teaches us about flexibility.
I keep the willow in mind when I think about
my journey. There have been really good times,
but there have also been really hard times.
And anywhere I go, I love being in nature.
Peace comes to me there, or I go find it.
The thing is, even nature deals with good times
and hard times. When I first started at the
garden, there was a big, beautiful willow tree—
and it fell down. It was so sad. But its roots
are deep, and it is growing back. It reminded
me that things might get hard, but peace will
come—or I can go find it. I'm still growing.*

CHANTAY ANDERSON
Nisqually, Nisqually Community Garden Program Manager

CHANTAY ANDERSON (B. 1994, SHE/HER) is a member of the Nisqually Indian Tribe located in Olympia, Washington. As the Nisqually Community Garden program manager, Anderson oversees the care and development of two properties that produce vegetables, berries, fruit trees, and some traditional plants. Annually, the garden produces over fifteen thousand pounds of food, which is distributed directly to Nisqually tribal members free of charge. The garden also hosts classes to make food and natural medicines, provides job training, offers youth field trips, and more. Anderson said the Nisqually Community Garden is a great example of tribal food sovereignty in action, because it makes a positive impact in the community while simultaneously flexing the Nisqually rights spelled out in the 1854 Treaty of Medicine Creek. Anderson is a 2017 graduate of Evergreen State College, where she studied photography and botany.

Everything I do reflects my legacy to place. The art I make. The wood I carve. The treaty and environmental laws I fight for—these are all the living breath of my ancestors. Mine is an ageless perspective of living in a space for multiple generations, times eons. What we do is a manifestation of who we are and where we come from, so we must do it with our whole self. It must be in our policy work, in protecting our cultural resources and traditional foods and ceremonies and all the species we maintain relations with. This is the literacy of our territory: who and what we are responsible for, to keep everything in balance.

MICAH HAWTWILTHIYATOOK MCCARTY
Makah, Tribal Leader and Artist

◄◆►

MICAH HAWTWILTHIYATOOK MCCARTY (B. 1970, HE/HIM) is a member of the Makah Tribe of Neah Bay, Washington. He was elected to tribal council in 2003 and served three consecutive, three-year terms—one of those terms as chairman. During his time on council, McCarty traveled to Belgium, Russia, and Japan and met both diplomats and whalers. He served on the Obama administration's National Ocean Council, the Biden administration's Council of Environmental Quality, and continues to serve on the Makah Whaling Commission, which he's advocated for since 1995, following in the footsteps of his father, the commission's first executive director. While McCarty has remained focused on Makah sovereignty, whaling and fishing rights, environmental protections, and international climate justice, he is also a master carver and a renowned artist who has revived traditional Makah art forms. McCarty carves functional canoes, massive totems, ceremonial masks, intricate puppets, and tribal regalia and instruments. He mentors and teaches younger generations to create traditional art forms.

Historically speaking, women never kept [themselves] in a box, not until colonizers told us our religions and practices were illegal, and they saw our empowered women as a threat. Living a healthy lifestyle is about women waking up our ancestral muscle memories. I hope that by showing others they can be proud and bold and beautiful in their own skin, that [they see it] is enough to empower your own people. Moving your body can help keep you safe and make your ancestors proud. And it's not just ancestors behind me. It's everyone: My cousins, sisters, everyone on the rez. I have no choice but to keep moving.

KOLA TUMHIYA SHIPPENTOWER
Cayuse, nimíipuu, Samoan, MMA Fighter, Football Player, MMIP Advocate, and Actress

KOLA TUMHIYA SHIPPENTOWER (B. 1989, SHE/HER) is Cayuse, nimíipuu, and Samoan. She is a member of the Confederated Tribes of the Umatilla Indian Reservation in Oregon. A survivor of domestic violence and sexual assault, Shippentower is known as a fierce advocate for Missing and Murdered Indigenous Peoples. In 2021, she founded the Wisáwca Project to help clients create a personalized safety plan and learn self-defense skills. A mother of three boys under fifteen, she's also a professional MMA fighter with a brown belt in Brazilian Jiu Jitsu. In 2024, Shippentower became the first Native American player to sign with the Oregon Ravens, the state's tackle football team for women and nonbinary players—a team since 2017. She also models and played the role of Keech in the independent film *Gift of Fear* (2023).

DONELLA MILLER (B. 1974, SHE/HER) is a member of the Confederated Tribes and Bands of the Yakama Nation and was selected to lead the Columbia River Inter-Tribal Fish Commission's Fishery Science Department in 2023. She is also a descendant of the Confederated Tribes of the Umatilla Indian Reservation and the Blackfeet Nation. The department Miller leads is tasked with increasing the scientific knowledge about Columbia River Basin fish and the habitats those fish rely on, which are threatened by industrialization, overconsumption, pollution, invasive species, and climate change. Miller's team provides valuable research to tribal, state, and federal management agencies while increasing the visibility of Indigenous scientific accomplishments. Miller said her interest in natural and cultural resources began as soon as she could explore; she was taught at an early age that her tribe considered themselves "salmon people," and she learned to sustain herself by fishing and foraging and to be responsible for her land, water, and non-human relatives. She started working for Yakama Fisheries when she turned eighteen.

People have this perspective that tribes only care about one thing. But we're not single-interest people. No one is. Yes, we care about fish, but it's not just about fish. It's not just about tearing out dams. Our tribal position is to set aside differences, to work together with everyone, to find collaborative and comprehensive solutions in environmentally conscious ways. We cannot keep disproportionately placing the burden on our sacred resources and our people, like the salmon, which is the core of our tribal culture, and the water, which is essential to all life on this earth. Let's not let the mistakes of the past define the outcomes for future generations.

DONELLA MILLER
Yakama, Umatilla, Blackfeet, Columbia River Inter-Tribal Fish Commission's Fishery Science Department Lead

Being Native is central to how I understand and act in the world. Growing up in my community, in Tulalip, surrounded by my extended family, I was raised and taught to be a good person and to always give back—more *us and we,* than *I and me.* . . . What motivates me every day is my passion to make change for the wellbeing of our children by breaking the cycle of misrepresentation, erasure, and systemic racism that has plagued our communities for generations and to pave the way for a more equitable and inclusive society in this country. Through applied, culturally grounded science, we continue the work of our ancestors to strengthen tribal sovereignty, empower our communities, and foster a brighter, more just future for Native peoples.

DR. STEPHANIE A. FRYBERG
Tulalip Tribes, Psychologist and Researcher

◀◆▶

DR. STEPHANIE A. FRYBERG (B. 1971, SHE/HER) is a member of the Tulalip Tribes of Washington. She received her master's and doctorate degrees in social psychology from Stanford University and was inducted into Stanford's Multicultural Hall of Fame in 2011. Her work bridges the fields of social and cultural psychology and Indigenous studies, and she has led groundbreaking studies on the use of Native mascots and other inaccurate representations of Native cultures. In these studies, the science underscores the intertwined nature of erasure, racism, and the detrimental impacts on Native peoples' well-being. Among many recognitions, Dr. Fryberg has received elected membership to the American Academy of Arts and Sciences (2023) and the Distinguished Service to the Field award from the Society for the Psychological Study of Social Issues. She founded the Research for Indigenous Social Action and Equity Center, a multidisciplinary collaborative dedicated to undoing Indigenous inequalities, conducting rigorous research to understand Indigenous experiences, and uplift Indigenous voices.

This is what brings me joy: when we have a ceremony, such as the first salmon ceremony, and we recognize the water and animal beings, the plant beings, the water itself and the land, and we remember our ancestors, and the gathering of people. This is what brings joy: as we return the salmon bones to the river for the continued return of the salmon; how a young child learns to peel hazel, and they want to show you what they did; the natural talent of our artists, and how they present and see our culture; when our elders get to use a digging stick to dig camas for the first time. . . . We get to say *ntsayka miłayt* (we are alive) to each new moon, just as our ancestors did.

GREG ARCHULETA
Willamette Tumwater, Clackamas and Watlala Chinook, Santiam Kalapuya, and Shasta/Takelma, Cultural Policy Analyst, Artist

GREG ARCHULETA (B. 1960, HE/HIM) is Willamette Tumwater, Clackamas and Watlala Chinook, Santiam Kalapuya, and Shasta/Takelma. He is a member of the Confederated Tribes of the Grand Ronde Community of Oregon where he is the cultural policy analyst. His work takes him across his tribe's ancestral lands, which include southwestern Washington, western Oregon, and northern California. Archuleta provides tribal members opportunities to access first foods, plants for basketry, and lands and waters for other cultural purposes. He also works with the United States Forest Service to manage a camas prairie in the Willamette National Forest, where he monitors the plants, helps remove invasive species, and advocates for controlled burns to help maintain the prairie as Indigenous people have done for thousands of years. In 2005, Archuleta created the Lifeways classes for off-reservation urban Natives to access cultural resources; today's classes include teachings related to art forms and the first foods of Indigenous peoples and communities. Archuleta is a celebrated artist known for his carvings, cedar hat-making, and other fine cultural creations.

This moment requires us to elevate and strengthen the voices of tribal leaders to coordinate, collaborate, and participate in local, national, and international adaptation and sustainability strategy planning.... Tribal Nations have nurtured, lived, and thrived on the lands of Turtle Island since time immemorial. Our cultures, traditions, lifestyles, communities, foods, treaty rights, and economies are inextricably linked to our ability to manage these natural resources.

FAWN SHARP
Quinault, Tribal Leader, Attorney, and Former President of the National Congress of American Indians

FAWN SHARP (B. 1970, SHE/HER) is a member of the Quinault Indian Nation in Washington, where she served five terms as tribal president and one as vice president. Sharp also served as the twenty-third president of the National Congress of American Indians (NCAI), the oldest and largest American Indian/Alaska Native tribal government organization in the United States. Sharp is the third woman to hold the position of NCAI president. She also served two terms as president of the Affiliated Tribes of Northwest Indians. Her past positions for the Quinault tribe include managing attorney, staff, attorney, lead counsel, and tribal court associate judge. She was also an administrative law judge for the Washington State Department of Revenue—Tax Appeals Division, and counsel for Phillips, Krause & Brown.

Fire is step zero in creating a relationship with the space around you. There are many steps after that, but having fire be the cultivator for existence is a wonderful feeling—like medicine. Fire strikes fear in a lot of people, but if Western society would acknowledge Indigenous understandings about prescription burns as the science it is, we'd have a lot less of these out-of-control wildfires. The rhetoric of fire as an enemy that must be suppressed is off. We should be using fire as an honored, ceremonial tool.

JAE VILES, SILETZ
Chinook, Educator/Practitioner of Cultural Burns

◀◆▶

JAE VILES (B. 1999, HE/HIM) is a member of the Confederated Tribes of Siletz Indians of Oregon and a descendant of the Joshua People of the Rogue River, the Sixes People of the Sixes River, and the Pillar Rock Chinook People of the Columbia River. Viles is a member of the Willamette Valley Fire Collaboration Crew, and in 2022, he helped establish the Wagon Burners, an all-Indigenous cultural burn crew based in Kalapuya Illahee (Willamette Valley) that works to reclaim Indigenous practices of cultural burning, uplifting Indigenous-led stewardship, and burning down the concepts of pioneer worship based on false histories. Viles is also a crew leader with Wisdom of the Elders, Inc., a nonprofit archive initiative where Viles teaches traditional ecological knowledge to youth, runs a tractor on a field of scotch broom, seeds riparian zones, and works with cultural and prescribed fires. Viles was born and raised in the Willamette Valley gathering beargrass, spruce root, cedar bark, hazel, nettles, mussels, crab, fish, mushrooms, huckleberries, and camas.

For me, performing and getting to clown as Carla is how I honor who I am as a Two Spirit person. The reason I perform, the reason I clown, is because it is medicine for the community and those I share Carla with, because together we're confronting issues of gender, race, class, environment—all of it—head-on, and we're doing so in a place that depowers those issues and confronts the flaws of an oppressive system. With Carla, it also becomes a space where we can laugh. And laughter is healing.

ANTHONY HUDSON/CARLA ROSSI
Grand Ronde, Siletz, Artist, Writer, and Drag Clown

ANTHONY HUDSON (B. 1986, ANY/ALL) is a citizen of the Confederated Tribes of Grand Ronde and a descendant of the Confederated Tribes of Siletz Indians. Hudson is an award-winning artist and writer who tours internationally as drag clown Carla Rossi (she/her). Hudson's performance work—from their award-winning solo stage show *Looking for Tiger Lily* to their role in the LGBTQ+ horror screening series known as *Queer Horror* at the Hollywood Theatre—has earned him international engagements, including Jeffrey Gibson's drag clown in residence at the 2024 Venice Biennale, features in *Hyperallergic and Art in America*, and sainthood from the Portland Sisters of Perpetual Indulgence. Hudson's writing has appeared in *American Theatre, BOMB Magazine*, and *Arts and International Affairs*. Carla Rossi started as Hudson's art project in 2010. Carla is a "drag clown," not a "drag queen," because Hudson intentionally utilizes Coyote-style trickery versus trying to emulate femininity. Carla—who lives in a dumpster behind the 7-Eleven—is a tool for critique, a clown who wears whiteface as a critical inversion of blackface, and a mirror reflecting artist and audience privilege.

59

XELI'TIA TEMRYSS LANE (B. 1982, SHE/HER) is from the Golden Eagle Clan of the Lummi Nation, a Coast Salish tribe in Washington. Lane played soccer professionally, semi-professionally, and collegiately as a defender for Balinge IF (Damallsvenskan, Uppsala, Sweden), Ajax of America, the California Storm, Arizona State University (ASU), and the U23 United States national team. Her experience brought her on global adventures in North America, Central America, South America, Africa, the Caribbean, and the Pacific Islands. Playing soccer led to a career in sports broadcasting; she became a journalist and analyst for the likes of Fox Soccer, Fox Sports, beIN SPORTS, and the Major League Soccer and Pac-12 networks. Lane is the vice president of Indian Country at Pyramid Communications, a Seattle-based public affairs and strategic communications firm. She holds a master's degree in American Indian studies from the University of California, Los Angeles, and a bachelor's degree from ASU in sociology and communications. Lane is a Nike N7 Ambassador and serves on several boards, including the Chief Seattle Club and Hummingbird Indigenous Family Services.

I want the next generations to
have the confidence to know they
are worthy of blazing trails
in any space, along any path of
their choosing. And I want them
to know they are never alone.
Call on your ancestors. Remember
where you come from.

XELI'TIA TEMRYSS LANE
*Lummi, Former Professional Soccer Player, Sports Journalist,
and Communications Expert*

Since Tribal programs and services are funded with non-defense discretionary appropriations, the funding levels are severely deficient and unable to address our Tribal communities' unmet needs; and these unfulfilled Federal obligations continue to grow exponentially on an annual basis. As a result, American Indians and Alaska Natives... continue to rank near the bottom of all Americans in terms of health, education, and employment status. These harrowing statistics and funding inequities demand a shift in the current governmental appropriations paradigm, not only because it is the right thing to do, but because it fails to align with the legally enforceable fiduciary obligation on the part of the United States to protect Tribal treaty rights, lands, resources, and assets.

W. RON ALLEN
S'Klallam, Tribal Chairman/CEO Jamestown S'Klallam Tribe

◄◆►

W. RON ALLEN (B. 1947, HE/HIM) has served as the Jamestown S'Klallam Tribal Chairman/CEO since 1977. Allen is responsible for leading his nation from a zero-resource base in 1982, to a current annual budget level of over $150 million via successful tribal enterprises, such as gaming, healthcare, infrastructure, food, entertainment, and cannabis, among many others. He is also credited with lifting his tribe out of landlessness; in 1982, the Jamestown S'Klallam reservation had zero land and today has amassed more than two thousand acres without federal assistance. In his nearly fifty years as leader, Allen has held several appointed and elected advisory positions under both White House party leaderships, including the Departments of Interior, Health and Human Services, Treasury, Justice, and State. Allen got a taste for tribal politics in the mid-1970s when, as a college student, he tried to get a replacement tribal ID and was denied because the tribe was no longer federally recognized. Allen was determined to help the tribe re-establish its federal status; after that success, Allen's community elected him to leadership and hasn't looked back.

History is very powerful, depending on who is telling the story. It can be used to demobilize a people or it can be used to inspire.

CHARLENE TETERS
Spokane, Celebrated Educator, Artist, and Activist

CHARLENE TETERS (B. 1952, SHE/HER) is a member of the Spokane Nation in Washington. She had a long and celebrated career as a faculty member at the Institute of American Indian Arts (IAIA) where she strove to shift the mainstream perception of Native people. Teters first gained national prominence as a graduate student at the University of Illinois Urbana-Champaign where she protested the sports teams' use of Indian mascots. The history of Teters' activism is the subject of the award-winning documentary *In Whose Honor?*, and she was a driving force behind the 2020 decision to rename the Washington NFL football team. Her art has been featured in over twenty major exhibitions, commissions, and collections. Teters earned all levels of fine arts degrees—associate, bachelor, master, and an honorary doctorate—from IAIA, the College of Santa Fe, the University of Illinois, and Mitchell College (Connecticut), respectively. Teters earned her associates from IAIA in 1984, joined the staff there in 1992, and was named academic dean in 2015. She retired in 2020.

Roots and Relations

If the ancestors of the Eastern Woodlands were some of this continent's first people to experience settler colonialism, then they were also the first to plant the seeds of resistance and resilience so that today's relations might take root and flourish. These ancestors had the forethought to seal and bury heirloom seeds in clay pots for their descendants to find and replant generations later. They signed treaties and made devastating decisions on the slim chance a story, a song, or a dance might survive long enough to keep future heads held high. They experienced germ warfare, the Trail of Tears, countless massacres, and the Carlisle Indian School—and still they saw a future with relations like those in the following pages.

Contemplating the extent of injustices done to these Indigenous nations is a monumental undertaking, as the Eastern Woodlands is a region spanning the Atlantic coastline along the east, the Great Lakes to the north, and the Gulf of Mexico to the south. European diseases devastated entire tribal nations—Washington, D.C., Manhattan, and Detroit, for instance, were once thriving Indigenous gathering places. Thrivance—the act of not just surviving, but flourishing— continues for the voices herein: a history-making Chief, Broadway and Hollywood actors, and a scholar of the highest merit, all rooted in the strength of their homelands, families, and passions.

Despite the many contributions modern society owes to the peoples of the Eastern Woodlands—genius gardening hacks and the United States Constitution, for instance—colonial history remembers these tribes with mythological feasts or disembodied Indian heads staked atop sports jerseys. The voices representing the Eastern Woodlands showcase why their nations deserve recognition for so much more: Their experiences inspire intentional, more purposeful relationships with our Afro-Indigenous kin, our bodies, community and capitalism, and plant and food systems.

Whether we are seed keepers, farmers, foragers, or home cooks, practicing and preserving our foodways makes us historians and cultural memory keepers, passing on the stories of how our people and our more-than-human kin have evolved through millennia together on this shared landmass. Every time we learn a new recipe, plant a seed, and feast together we are helping to transmit knowledge, technologies, and skills from one generation to the next—just as others did for us. And each time an Indigenous person tends a garden, cooks, and eats their ancestral foods, it is an act of resistance and love, a reclamation of identity, and a proud declaration that we will always be here.

SHILOH MAPLES
Odawa, Ojibwe, Food Sovereignty Advocate

SHILOH MAPLES (B. 1986, SHE/THEY) is Odawa and Ojibwe and a citizen of the Little River Band of Ottawa Indians of Michigan. Maples earned a master's degree in social work from the University of Michigan, where she specialized in community organizing. They also completed programs in organic farming and sustainable community design. Maples partnered with Detroit's Indigenous community for nearly ten years to develop Sacred Roots, a food sovereignty initiative that increased access to ancestral foods, offered culturally based nutrition education, and created opportunities for the community to practice cultural foodways. As part of this initiative, Maples taught gardening, seed saving, and cooking classes that promoted using traditional, seasonal, and local foods to improve participants' health while reconnecting them with their culture. Maples was a writer-in-residence at Denniston Hill in upstate New York in 2021; a year later, they partnered with Whetstone Media to launch Spirit Plate, a podcast where Maples discussed the social, political, and historical aspects of Indigenous food sovereignty and uplifted the movement's seed keepers, chefs, historians, and community members.

The truth is, identity isn't about choosing. It's about being. And sometimes, the world can feel lonely and dark when you refuse to fit into the boxes others create for you.... I've learned to appreciate who I am, even in solitude, because sometimes, you have to walk alone to find the community truly meant for you. When I think about seeing my own light, I think about seeing me—beyond labels, beyond expectations.... Who are you? What is your relationship with yourself? That's your light. That's how you truly shine from the inside out. In Shinnecock, we greet each other with *Aquay*. It means "hello," but its deeper meaning is "I see the light in you." Aquay—I see the light in you. Do you see the light in yourself?

AUTUMN ROSE MISKWEMINANOCSQUA WILLIAMS
Shinnecock, Black, Motivational Speaker, Model, and Communications Professional

◄ ◆ ►

AUTUMN ROSE MISKWEMINANOCSQUA (RASPBERRY STAR WOMAN) WILLIAMS (B. 1993, SHE/HER) is a passionate advocate for Indigenous and multicultural communities. Her expertise in public relations and communications is used to amplify underrepresented voices, social justice initiatives, mental health awareness, and cultural representation. Born and raised on the Shinnecock Reservation in Southampton, New York, Williams served as Miss Native American United States from 2017 to 2018 and used her platform to elevate Indigenous visibility and empowerment. Since then, Williams has led strategic communications efforts for many organizations, including the Shinnecock Nation, the Administration for Native Americans, ICF Next, and Agency MABU. Williams has facilitated powerful conversations on Afro-Indigenous identity, body positivity, and mental health at high-profile venues, such as American University, Muckleshoot Tribal School, Google's John E. Martin Mental Healthcare Symposium, and the Mental Health America Conference.

There were lots of times growing up I didn't feel like I was enough. As an Afro-Indigenous person, a mixed person, no matter what room I stepped in, I got looks, you know? But it was my cultures—my Seaconke Wampanoag side and my Cape Verdean side, my mom's side, my dad's side, all my sides— that helped me celebrate who I was. When you dig down deep into family and community, you realize you don't have to prove anything to anyone. In all my histories, my people were warriors. I have a resilient heritage. . . . So now I look at being mixed, like, this is dope! I'm not looking for outside acceptance; I look to my people for that. It's not about me—it's about we.

KALI REIS
Seaconke Wampanoag, Cape Verdean, Actress and Boxer

KALI REIS (B. 1986, SHE/HER/THEY) is a member of the Seaconke Wampanoag tribe and also of Cherokee and Nipmuc ancestry on her mother's side. Her father is of Cape Verdean ancestry. In 2024, Reis became the first Afro-Indigenous and Two Spirit (queer) person to be nominated for an Emmy Award for their supporting role as Evangeline Navarro in HBO/Max's crime series *True Detective: Night Country* (2024). Reis made her film debut in the 2021 Tribeca Film Festival award-winning *Catch the Fair One*, which she also co-wrote; that performance earned Reis a nomination for Best Female Lead Independent Spirit Award. Before acting, there was boxing: Reis held the World Boxing Council female middleweight title in 2016, and the World Boxing Association, World Boxing Organization, and International Boxing Organization female light welterweight titles between 2020 and 2022. Reis uses the nickname K.O. Mequinonoag (many feathers/many talents); she was inducted into the North American Indigenous Athletics Hall of Fame in 2022. Reis passionately advocates for Missing and Murdered Indigenous Women and Girls and mentors at-risk young people.

DR. KYLE T. MAYS (B. 1987, HE/HIS) is Afro-Indigenous and a member of the Saginaw Chippewa Tribe of Michigan. He is an award-winning writer and scholar of United States history, urban studies, race relations, and contemporary popular culture. He is a tenured associate professor in the Department of African American Studies, the Department of American Indian Studies, and the Department of History at the University of California, Los Angeles. Dr. Mays is the author of *Hip Hop Beats, Indigenous Rhymes: Modernity and Hip Hop in Indigenous North America* (2018), *An Afro-Indigenous History of the United States* (2021), *City of Dispossessions: Indigenous Peoples, African Americans, and the Creation of Modern Detroit* (2022), and *Rethinking the Red Power Movement* (co-written with Sam Hitchmough, 2024). Dr. Mays earned his bachelor's degree in social relations and policy from James Madison College in 2009, and his master's degree (2012) and doctorate (2015) in American history from the University of Illinois Urbana-Champaign.

A phrase I live by is *mino-bimaadiziwin*, which translates to "the good life." For me, having family, comrades, and creating kinship is the good life.... I want to become a good ancestor, and a part of that is people seeing me as a flawed human who tried to educate as many people as I could. I failed, I succeeded, but I hope the next generation will take my work, expand on it, and do it better than me. But ultimately, I hope they understand that I cared and dared to imagine Black and Indigenous futures as a core part of becoming a good ancestor. I truly believe that if these communities— my ancestry—came together, we would change the material conditions of our lives. And I hope the next generation makes this happen.

DR. KYLE T. MAYS
Afro-Indigenous, Saginaw Chippewa, Writer and Scholar

Getting to exist as a Native in my full truth in an iconic story like *The Outsiders* on Broadway has given me hope that directors will continue to cast Native and mixed Native talent for roles that have historically been inaccessible to us. Being able to lend my voice to Spirit Rangers with actors from so many other different tribes made me feel extremely seen; I'm reminded that teaching our young people the importance of our cultures ensures those identities and that knowledge will be strong for generations to come.

SKY LAKOTA-LYNCH
Haliwa-Saponi, Broadway Actor

◄◆►

SKY LAKOTA-LYNCH (B. 1991, HE/HIM) is Haliwa-Saponi and Ethiopian. He was nominated for a Tony Award in 2024 for his incredible performance as Johnny Cade in the Broadway musical adaptation of *The Outsiders*, which took home the 2024 Tony Award for Best Musical. Fun fact: The character of Johnny is also Native, and his costume is embroidered with the colors of the Haliwa-Saponi Nation. Lakota-Lynch graduated from the Neighborhood Playhouse School of the Theatre and made his acting debut in the short film *Contagion* (2009). He had guest roles on several TV and streaming shows, including *Iron Fist*, *Spirit Rangers*, and *Foul Play*. Lakota-Lynch made his stage debut as Jared Kleinman on Broadway's *Dear Evan Hansen*.

Native peoples have endured many injustices as a result of federal policy, including federal actions that sought to terminate Tribal Nations, assimilate Native people, and to erode Tribal territories, learning, and cultures. This story involves the cession of vast land holdings and natural resources, oftentimes by force, to the United States, out of which grew an obligation to provide benefits and services—promises made to Tribal Nations that exist in perpetuity. These resources are the very foundation of this nation and have allowed the United States to become the wealthiest and strongest world power in history. Federal appropriations and services to Tribal Nations and Native people are simply a repayment on this perpetual debt.

CHIEF MUTĀWI MUTĀHASH MARILYNN "LYNN" MALERBA
Mohegan, United States Treasurer and Chief of the Mohegan Tribe

MOHEGAN CHIEF MUTĀWI MUTĀHASH (MANY HEARTS) MARILYNN "LYNN" MALERBA (B. 1953, SHE/HER) became the first Native American woman to have her signature appear on United States currency when President Joe Biden appointed her United States Treasurer in 2022, a role that directly oversees the United States Mint, the Bureau of Printing and Engraving, and storage of about $270 billion worth of gold at Fort Knox. Malerba became the eighteenth Chief of the Mohegan Tribe in 2010 and is the first female Chief in the tribe's modern history. The position is a lifetime appointment made by the tribe's Council of Elders. She previously served in tribal government for many years and had a long medical career, ultimately serving as the director of cardiology and pulmonary services at Lawrence + Memorial Hospital in Connecticut. Malerba earned a bachelor's degree in nursing from the College of St. Joseph and master's degree in public administration from the University of Connecticut. Later, she earned a Doctor of Nursing Practice at Yale University and was named a Jonas Scholar.

The policies and assimilation practices of the United States had the sole purpose of culturally assimilating American Indian, Alaska Native, and Native Hawaiian children at residential boarding schools across the country. Children were coerced, and many times, compelled to attend boarding schools away from their home. Many children did not return to their families or their communities. Those that did return lost generations' worth of cultural knowledge, stories, and traditions; and communities lost their language keepers, cultural practitioners, and future leaders. . . . If Native children were able to endure and survive the Indian Boarding School era in our nation, then we should be able to find it in ourselves to fully investigate what happened to our relatives and work towards a brighter path for the next seven generations.

SHARICE DAVIDS
Ho-Chunk, Politician, Attorney, Athlete, and Author

SHARICE DAVIDS, HO-CHUNK (B. 1980, SHE/HER), is a citizen of the Ho-Chunk Nation of Wisconsin. She is the first openly gay member of Congress to represent Kansas and helped to draft the bipartisan-sponsored Truth and Healing Commission on Indian Boarding School Policies Act of 2021. Advocating for ancestors and relatives who were victims and survivors of boarding schools has been a priority for Davids, whose grandparents were both survivors of such schools. Davids was born in Frankfurt, Germany— her mother served twenty years in the United States Army. She earned a law degree from Cornell Law School and served as a White House Fellow under President Barack Obama, which led to her interest in politics. In 2018, Davids defeated a four-term incumbent in a United States House race to represent Kansas, and she continues the fight to limit the influence of special interests and make healthcare more affordable and accessible to everyone. In 2021, Davids wrote a children's picture book, *Sharice's Big Voice: A Native Kid Becomes a Congresswoman*. Before taking office, Davids competed as an amateur mixed martial arts fighter.

The Oneida language is a key component of our cultural identity. Language is medicine, and when we use *kanukwatslyo*, the good medicine of our language, we begin to heal our students and community.

TEHASSI TASI HILL
Oneida, Leader and Land, Language, and Sovereignty Advocate

◄◆►

TEHASSI TASI HILL (B. 1980, HE/HIM) is Oneida and was elected chairman for the Oneida Nation in Wisconsin in 2017. He serves on the Oneida Business Committee, the Great Lakes Inter-Tribal Council, and the Natural Resources Damage Trustee Council, and is a designee to Environmental Protection Agency's Regional Tribal Operating Committee. Hill is known for successfully leading his nation through several high-profile challenges, including the COVID-19 pandemic and a victory upholding the Indian Child Welfare Act in the United States Supreme Court. Rooting his priorities in language revitalization, land reclamation, and tribal self-determination has helped him earn the trust and votes of his relations on the reservation where he was born and raised. Hill studied business administration at the University of Wisconsin at Green Bay and operated a successful painting business prior to working in government.

It doesn't matter what language or what tribe you're from. It's important that we emphasize our culture, and our culture is very important . . . If we take care of our culture, our language, and our identity, we take care of sovereignty.

ROBERT VANZILE, JR.
Sokaogon Ojibwe, Educator, Culture and Language Preservationist, Tribal Leader

ROBERT VANZILE, JR. (B. 1955, HE/HIM) is Sokaogon Ojibwe and Tribal Council Chairman of the Sokaogon Chippewa Community, Mole Lake Band of Lake Superior Chippewa in Wisconsin. VanZile was appointed to the Interior Department's Advisory Council for Climate Adaptation Science. Before joining the tribal council, he was a dedicated teacher at the Indian Community School in Milwaukee and maintains a firm foothold for education advocacy. In 2021, VanZile led a campaign to install traditional place names on Wisconsin's road signs. In 2023, the state's transportation department unveiled a new, bright green sign pointing Highway 55 drivers toward VanZile's reservation: *Zaaga'inganiin*, which means "place of light in the water."

CHARLES NORMAN SHAY (B. 1924, HE/HIM) is a member of the Penobscot Nation in Maine. He is a tribal elder, writer, and decorated veteran of both World War II and the Korean War. Along with a Bronze Star and Silver Star, Shay was also awarded the Legion d'Honneur, making him the first Native American in Maine with the distinction of French chevalier. Shay's autobiography, *Project Omaha Beach: The Life and Military Service of a Penobscot Indian Elder* (2012), details his experiences being drafted into the military in 1943 at the age of nineteen. He was a WWII combat medic during many battles and he reenlisted with the Army in 1950 to serve as a combat medic in the Korean War, noting the few employment opportunities available to him. Shay exemplifies the dedication Native Americans have shown to military campaigns since the founding of the United States: Native people serve in the United States Armed Forces at five times the national average and have served in every major United States conflict for more than two hundred years, despite not receiving citizenship until 1924.

The Penobscot Indian has participated in all wars beginning with the Revolutionary War … Our ancestors never evaded the opportunity to offer their services to the democratic government of the United States in time of war… Many of our ancestors paid the ultimate price and many others returned maimed and disabled…. The experience of participating in the military service during war time has had a deep lying effect on our lives as any Veteran will tell you. Many experiences are sometimes hard to forget. The time has come when we need to help and do what we can for our veterans and their dependents.

CHARLES NORMAN SHAY, PENOBSCOT
WWII and Korean War Veteran

Innovators and Influencers

◀◆▶

The nations and people representing the Southern/Southeastern tribes of the United States and the Caribbean have accomplished extraordinary firsts in their respective fields. Their work has led to innovations in ancestry connections. These voices have influenced United States Supreme Court Justices, Hollywood film directors, NASA spaceships, and bestseller lists.

The Southern and Southeastern tribes represented in this sequence include those whose original homelands range from North Carolina south to the Caribbean, west through Texas, and north through Oklahoma. While there is regional overlap with the Great Plains, the voices in this sequence are descended from nations with southern origin histories; for instance, the Cherokee, Chickasaw, Choctaw, Creek, and Seminole were displaced further and further west by colonial and genocidal endeavors since the time of first European contact. Who better to represent innovation than tribes forced to reinvent the ways and means to survive? A bestselling young adult author in Texas uses their background as a geoscientist and oceanographer to research and analyze data to advocate for their tribe's land and treaty rights, while a tribal leader in Florida took a chance and gambled that a sports betting app would pay off big time—it did.

For many years, non-Indigenous government officials, researchers, and anthropologists believed the Taíno people extinct. A voice highlighted in this sequence, and her innovative digital application, is proof to the contrary, and she ensures future Taíno voices will be documented, connected, and heard. Alongside this Taíno creator are other Southern innovators and influencers who prove they are more than fodder for history books.

PRISCILLA BELL LAMBERTY (B. 1972, SHE/HER) is a Black and Borikua Taíno muralist, painter, educator, and community builder. In 2024, Lamberty was named a finalist for the prestigious MIT Solve Indigenous Communities Fellowship. Her nonprofit, the Borikua Taíno Foundation, proposed a digital platform for Borikua Taíno descendants to enroll, connect, and celebrate heritage through a mobile app called Yucayekeno Connect, a secure and user-friendly way to map Borikén's Taíno legacy, reconnect with community and culture, and document descendancy via a centralized platform. As an artist, Lamberty's work centers on themes of identity and cultural heritage. Lamberty earned her master's degree in fine arts from Moor College of Art and Design. She received the Leeway Art and Change grant (2017), the Taíno Storyteller of the Year award (2017), the Taíno Muralist of the Year award (2020), and the Leeway Transformation Award (2023), among others. Lamberty's art is celebrated for its exploration of issues related to parenthood, environmental justice, the centering and uplifting of Black and brown voices in colonial spaces, and Indigenous/Native and Indigenous Caribbean visibility.

Much of my work focuses on educating my own people. I mean, we were the very first contact peoples—that's 532 years of colonialism. Some other Native nations' first contact with Europeans and colonization is much more recent—still devastating, of course—but it's a difference of two hundred, three hundred years. The ongoing erasure of the Taíno is what 532 years looks like. Today, many Taíno descendants don't identify as Indigenous Caribbean, they may infantilize, tokenize, or worse, reject their Indigenous heritage entirely. Personally, art helps me heal ancestral trauma. . . . It honors my Ancestors, those whose contributions are often left unacknowledged from the stories, culture, and language of the Caribbean. The Taíno who had to hide their identities to survive deserve to have their stories told.

PRISCILLA BELL LAMBERTY
Borikua Taíno, Black, Muralist, Painter, Educator, and Community Builder

Gadugi. In Cherokee, this is a value we hold near and dear. Essentially, it means "we do what we can for our community." It's more than just community service. It reflects the reality that our lives are inextricably linked to one another. . . . At times, it can feel like nothing we do makes a difference. But gadugi also reminds us that we are not alone. Our community is working and fighting right alongside us. We don't have to worry about doing it all. We just have to do our part. And that is what I strive to do each and every day: My part. I don't always succeed, and sometimes I fall short. But it's a goal and a comfort to know we abide by this traditional principle.

MARY KATHRYN NAGLE
Cherokee, Attorney at Law, Playwright, and Screenwriter

MARY KATHRYN NAGLE (B. 1983, SHE/HER) is an enrolled citizen of the Cherokee Nation of Oklahoma. She is a renowned playwright and attorney specializing in the sovereignty of Native nations and peoples. She is celebrated for her work to end violence against Native women. Nagle has penned more than fifteen plays; *Sliver of a Full Moon* has been performed in law schools from Stanford to Harvard. She worked extensively on the reauthorization of the Violence Against Women Act and has filed numerous briefs in the United States Supreme Court as a part of the National Indigenous Women's Resource Center's VAWA Sovereignty Initiative. In 2013, Nagle filed an amicus brief in *Adoptive Couple v. Baby Girl* (the Baby Veronica case). Nagle received her bachelor's degree from Georgetown University and her law degree from Tulane University Law School; Nagle clerked for two federal judges in the United States District Court for the District of Nebraska. In law school, Nagle began advocating for Native rights as a playwright. She has a producer credit for the hit Hulu film *Prey* (2022).

*My ancestors were on a journey,
a migration led by two brothers who
split apart and followed a vision to
do what was best for their people.
This happens throughout Chickasaw
history with our leaders making
tough decisions. When I reflect on
what my ancestors did, their
decisions, against all the odds, allowed
me to flourish. Allowed me to
walk the Earth. And walk above it.*

JOHN B. HERRINGTON
Chickasaw, Astronaut

COMMANDER JOHN B. HERRINGTON, PH.D. (B. 1958, HE/HIM), is an enrolled member of the Chickasaw Nation and a scientific storyteller. When he traveled to space as part of Space Shuttle Endeavour's STS-113 mission in 2002, Herrington became the first Native American in space. He logged over 330 hours in space, including three spacewalks, which are commemorated on the 2019 Sacagawea one dollar coin. Space wasn't where Herrington thought he would end up after his suspension from college as a freshman with a 1.72 GPA. The outdoors and rock climbing were more his speed, but with a mentor's help, Herrington connected mountaineering with measurements and angles, and he earned a degree in mathematics from the University of Colorado at Colorado Springs in 1983. He joined the United States Navy, excelled at flying, and earned a master's degree in aeronautical engineering from the United States Naval Postgraduate School in 1995. Herrington retired from the Navy and NASA in July 2005. He earned his Ph.D. in education from the University of Idaho in 2014 and wrote the children's book *Mission to Space* (2016).

I like to try to weave in humor to keep heavy subjects balanced, but also to show Native people being funny, both myself as a writer and my characters, because too many people get so serious and sad about our lives. And we really do like to laugh— I mean, everyone does—but for Native people that's sort of been taken away from us; we're stuck being stoic. . . . I hope to leave a body of work to future generations that can be helpful, that can enrich the lives of people living in the future. If we have one.

TOMMY ORANGE
Cheyenne, Arapaho, Author

TOMMY ORANGE (B. 1982, HE/HIM) is a citizen of the Cheyenne and Arapaho Tribes of Oklahoma and was raised in Oakland, California. He is the acclaimed and bestselling author of *There, There* (2018), a debut that received the 2018 John Leonard Prize, the 2019 PEN/Hemingway Award, and the 2019 American Book Award. Orange was also a finalist for the 2019 Pulitzer Prize. In 2024, Orange published *Wandering Stars*, which was longlisted for that year's Booker Prize, making Orange the first Native American to receive the honor. That same year, Orange was selected to contribute to the Future Library project, which invites a new author every year to produce a manuscript to be stored under lock and key until 2114. Orange is the eleventh writer to be asked to join the project, which began in 2014 by artist Katie Paterson; it will culminate in an anthology of a century's worth of secret works from authors such as Margaret Atwood, Tsitsi Dangarembga, Ocean Vuong, Karl Ove Knausgård, and Elif Shafak.

Every plate that comes out of our kitchen tells a different story. A beautiful story about the three sisters. A seasonal story about vibrant berries from our northern relatives. Tepary beans that tell a desert story that's a thousand years old. Our four-legged relatives are always telling us stories. The colors, the smells, the tastes, and then the knowledge that comes from each ingredient on that plate—the tribe that cultivated it, that sang to it, that danced for it—that's what we're feeding you. And it tastes really good. That's food sovereignty.

CHEF CRYSTAL WAHPEPAH
Kickapoo, Owner of Wahpepah's Kitchen

CHEF CRYSTAL WAHPEPAH (B. 1969, SHE/HER) is an enrolled member of the Kickapoo Nation of Oklahoma. She is an award-winning culinary artist who opened one of the nation's first Indigenous restaurants, Wahpepah's Kitchen, in Oakland in 2021, after owning a catering business for twelve years. Her first cookbook, *A Feather and a Fork*, is set to be published in 2025. Wahpepah's unique and exciting take on Indigenous cuisine made her a finalist for the 2022 Emerging Chef Award from the James Beard Foundation. In 2024, the foundation's Taste America culinary series kicked off its twenty-city tour in San Francisco to spotlight chefs like Wahpepah who are driving the food industry's evolution. Later that year, Hulu and Disney+ streamed the National Geographic special *Our America: A Queen's Journey*, in which Wahpepah was featured. In 2016, she was the first Native American chef to compete in the Food Network's show *Chopped*. For her work, Wahpepah received the Indigenous Artist Activist Award and was inducted into the Native American Almanac for being one of the first Native women to own a catering business.

MARCELLUS OSCEOLA JR. (B. 1972, HE/HIM) is Seminole and the current and seventh tribal council chairman of the Seminole Tribe of Florida. Known for his entrepreneurial skills, Osceola ran limousine, lawncare, and seafood companies before becoming chairman in 2017. As a leader, Osceola oversees a bold, thirty-year, multibillion-dollar gaming compact with Florida that gives his tribe control of sports betting throughout the state. Under the three-decade compact, the Seminoles agree to pay Florida about $20 billion, including $2.5 billion over the first five years. The deal also authorized the Seminoles to offer craps and roulette at their casinos and create a sports betting app for smart devices, and it green lights the construction of three casinos on tribal property. The tribe's competitors, fearful of losing revenue, took their worries all the way to the United States Supreme Court. In June 2024, the Court declined to take up the challenge, a huge victory for Osceola and his tribe. The decision could cement the tribe's control of sports betting indefinitely, as well as impact tribal gaming throughout Indian Country.

Seminoles have lived in Florida for thousands of years. When President Andrew Jackson signed into law the Indian Removal Act in 1830, we resisted efforts to displace us from our native lands. Instead, we settled deep into the Florida Everglades where we maintained our ways and traditions.... [T]oday we number more than four thousand Tribal members. We are a sovereign government with our own schools, police, and courts. We run one of the largest cattle operations in the United States. We own Hard Rock International, with locations in 74 countries. [We] continue our traditions of sewing, patchwork, chickee building, and alligator wrestling.... [T]he world has changed, as it always has; and we have adapted, as we always have.

MARCELLUS OSCEOLA JR.
Seminole, Chairman, Seminole Tribe of Florida

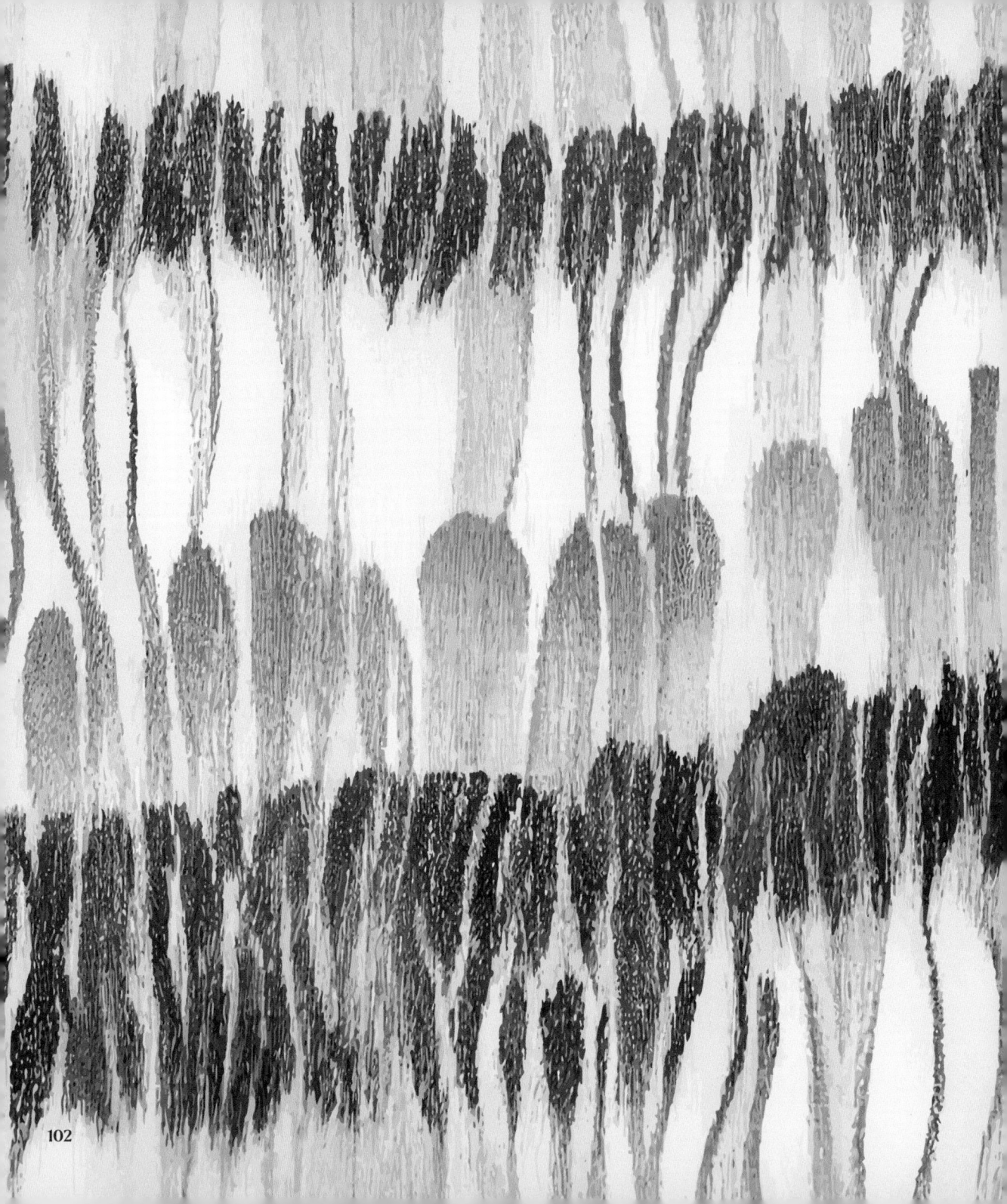

Tribal culture, economic growth, and food security are deeply rooted in agriculture, and so the Department of Agriculture shares an outsized responsibility to support our Tribal Nations, Alaska Natives and Native Hawaiians. . . . Complicated problems require complicated solutions, but USDA is eager to be a partner in driving economic growth in Native communities. It is critical that USDA supports Tribes in their efforts to restore and build food and economic sovereignty.

JANIE SIMMS HIPP
Chickasaw, Agricultural Legal Expert

JANIE SIMMS HIPP (B. 1955, SHE/HER) is an enrolled citizen of the Chickasaw Nation and was the first Native American to serve as general counsel at the United States Department of Agriculture; she was the most senior Native person to serve in the USDA in its 159-year history, and one of only four women to occupy the position since 1905. Hipp is the CEO/ president of Native Agriculture Financial Services. Hipp founded the USDA Office of Tribal Relations, the Indigenous Food and Agriculture Initiative, the Native American Agriculture Fund, and was a national program leader at the USDA National Institute for Food and Agriculture. She has a juris doctorate from Oklahoma City University School of Law and a master of laws in agricultural and food law from the University of Arkansas School of Law. Her many accolades include the Distinguished Service Award from the American Agricultural Law Association, the Volunteer Service Award for Lifetime Achievement from U.S. President Barack Obama, and the 2021 Congressional Hunger Center Trailblazer Hunger Leadership Award. Hipp was inducted into the Chickasaw Hall of Fame in 2024.

As children, we walk through landmine fields of cultural stereotypes that slander, smear, mock, or belittle our ancestors, heroes, leaders, families, friends and future generations. As Native nations, communities, organizations, and individuals, we help each other to address the actions that target us or to stay out of harm's way. Some of our peoples cannot or will not stand up for themselves—they shut down, avoid the issue, or, the saddest reaction of all, internalize the slurs and negative messages, and act out in self-destructive ways, or take aim against the nearest available target— so, those of us who can, stand up for those who can't and for each other.

SUZAN SHOWN HARJO
Cheyenne, Hotvlkvlke Mvskokvlke, and Nuyakv, Leader, Advocate, Writer

SUZAN SHOWN HARJO (B. 1945, SHE/HER) is a Cheyenne citizen, Hotvlkvlke Mvskokvlke, Nuyakv, and an enrolled member of the Cheyenne and Arapaho Tribes of Oklahoma. She is the first Native woman elected to the oldest learned societies in the United States: The American Academy of Arts and Sciences (2020 Fellow) and the American Philosophical Society (2022 Fellow). Harjo's distinguished career includes presiding over the Morning Star Institute since 1984. She is also the former executive director of the National Congress of American Indians and Native American Rights Fund and is a founding trustee of the Smithsonian National Museum of the American Indian. Critical legislation has her name on it, including the American Indian Religious Freedom Act of 1978, the National Museum of the American Indian Act of 1989, and the Native American Graves Protection and Repatriation Act of 1990. Harjo's advocacy extends to protections for Native identity, children, cultural rights, land, water, and sacred places, as well as the return of more than one million acres of Indigenous lands.

I'm not a scientist or a doctor; I am a tribal community member, who fully understands the toll diabetes has taken, reaching far beyond our tribal communities. . . . However, our story is not just one of suffering, misery and despair—it is also a story of great perseverance, determination and hope for the future. Across Indian Country, there are inspiring stories of elders, community leaders, women, men, and even children, who have been empowered with the knowledge and tools to effectively combat this disease. . . . The strength, courage, and resolve of these citizens rival any of the characters I have portrayed on the big screen.

WES STUDI
Cherokee, Academy Award-Honored Actor

WES STUDI (B. 1947, HE/HIM) is a citizen of the Cherokee Nation. In 2019, he became the first Native American to receive an Academy Award when he was presented with an Honorary Oscar. Studi is a seasoned actor and producer with roles in award-winning blockbuster films like *Dances with Wolves* and *Avatar*. He helped expand Native American representation in film and television with more than eighty credits to his name. Studi served in the United States Army during the Vietnam War. After his discharge, he became active in the Native American rights movement in the 1970s, then enrolled at Tulsa Community College where he began acting for the American Indian Theater Company. In addition to Hollywood and stage acting, Studi is passionate about using his platform to influence lawmakers and advocate for issues important to Indigenous communities, including understanding and preventing diabetes, a disease with near-zero degrees of separation for Native families in the United States.

Desert Heartwork

<figure>◄ ◆ ►</figure>

The desert has a lousy marketing department; the average person might visualize a dusty landscape full of hot and stingy ways to suffer dehydration. But the desert, like the voices in this sequence, is full of bounty, life, and heart. These voices are utilizing ancestral knowledge of plant relatives to create dryland farms, fields, and orchards in the high desert; they create communities on social media, in bookstores, on the pages of comics, in the imaginations of Indigenous children, and on urban bike paths; and they demand justice for the voices of their ancestors and today's oppressed relatives, so their children don't carry burdens, only love.

The voices of the Southwest region are from tribal nations in the current states of Colorado, Arizona, New Mexico, Utah, and Nevada in the western United States, and the states of Sonora and Chihuahua in northern Mexico. The voices descend from the brilliant architects of ancient, multistoried stone and adobe cities, mind-boggling cliff dwellings, and extensive irrigation canals—many of which are still used today in metropolitan cities like Phoenix, Arizona. Their ancestors also cultivated drought-tolerant staple foods, including tepary beans, maize, and squash, and harvested fruit from saguaro, cholla, and prickly pear cacti, all of which are widely farmed today and cooked in recipes to reconnect families to healthier first foods.

The deep passion of heartwork resonates within every voice of this sequence. Be it the history-making political speech that shines as brilliant and uninterrupted as the desert sky, or the fierce survival work of Indigenous imagination, the voices of this region speak of community, who builds it, where it comes together, and what keeps it going for future generations.

We have the responsibility to nurture an emergent Indigenous futurism that is joyful, abundant, accountable, transparent, equitable, and just. Our collective work is generational; we stand on the strong foundation of those who have come before, and it is our responsibility to ensure that our children, more-than-human relations, and future generations will have a safe, stable, secure, generative, and healthy future. I look forward to being part of the change that needs to happen so that those who come after will know that someone prayed for them to be here.

LILIAN HILL
Hopi, Quechan, Akimel O'odham, Founder of Hopi Tutskwa Permaculture

LILIAN HILL (B. 1980, SHE/HER) belongs to the Pipwungwa (Tobacco) Clan of the Hopi Tribe and is also of Quechan and Akimel O'odham descent. Hill founded Hopi Tutskwa Permaculture in 2004, an organization that rejuvenates Hopi culture and traditions through active community and youth engagement by integrating ancestral knowledge with modern techniques. Recognized for outstanding community leadership, strategic advising, and resource mobilizing, Hill has extensive expertise as a natural builder, land steward, and farmer. Hill studied at the North American School of Natural Building and earned degrees in applied Indigenous studies and traditional ecological knowledge from Northern Arizona University. Hill is a certified permaculture designer, natural builder, and a 2019 Castanea Fellow, a program that supports leaders working to create racially just food systems. Hill was awarded the 2015 Agricultural Humanitarian of the Year Award by the Justin Willie Foundation. Her deep connection to the land is evident as she forages and farms across mountains, mesas, and the lower Sonoran desert to foster plant relationships throughout the Colorado Plateau and beyond.

I'm always interested in one's relationship to the land. I believe everyone is the product of our ecosystem and our ancestors, and whether I'm on my bike, or running, that connection to being outside with the land is so healing. . . . Community endeavors are all about connections and sprinkling seeds without really knowing what will grow from it. I'm an ideas person who tries to meet people where they are. I will care for you and watch you grow into whatever you're going to grow into. If you flower, great. If you grow into a tree, then wow. The outcome is the outcome. I never want to assume anything about anyone. And that's usually where exciting and beautiful things happen.

GUARINA PALOMA LOPEZ
Pascua Yaqui/Yoeme, Founder of Native Women Ride

GUARINA PALOMA LOPEZ (B. 1979, SHE/HER/ELLA) is Yoeme and a member of the Pascua Yaqui Tribe of Tucson, Arizona. Lopez was one of nine people named *Bicycling* magazine's 2023 Riders of the Year after completing a 220-mile ride to raise awareness about the history and impact of Indian boarding schools. Lopez is a multimedia artist, photographer, and storyteller who founded Native Women Ride to connect with other Native/Indigenous bike riders, who have significantly low representation in the biking community. What started on Instagram during a pandemic lockdown in 2021 has grown to in-person meet-ups, ride groups, race groups, and community building across the nation with funding for Native/Indigenous peoples who identify as femme, trans, women, and/or nonbinary. The organization has now grown to include the Indigenous Cycling Collective, with funding for Native/Indigenous bike riders irrespective of gender identity, and Bright Path Collective, an endeavor for more athletic-minded riders. She was a 2023 recipient of a Storyknife Residency in Homer, Alaska.

DR. LEE FRANCIS 4 (B. 1977, HE/HIM) is from the Pueblo of Laguna in New Mexico and is the chief imagination officer of the Indigenous Imagination Workshop, an organization dedicated to sparking and cultivating the Indigenous imagination. An educator and entrepreneur, Dr. Francis is the founder of the Indigenous Comic Con, Indigenous Worlds of Wonder, the Indigenous Futurisms Festival, Native Realities, and Red Planet Books and Comics. He is an award-winning writer and editor with multiple publications from poetry to short stories to comics. He was the host and lead writer for *Indigi-Genius* on New Mexico PBS, the co-producer for *Sovereign Innovations* on PBS Digital, and the publisher for the award-winning media platform, A Tribe Called Geek. He also created *Sovereignty Gardens*, a Native American puppetry show for kids. Dr. Francis earned his Ph.D. in education from Texas State University in 2014; he worked for the Bureau of Indian Affairs in Washington, D.C., and the Pueblo of Laguna Department of Education. He also served as the national director of Wordcraft Circle, Inc., which focused on promoting stories as a means of cultural sustainability.

Indigenous imaginations aren't predicated upon object ownership. No, that's colonial intention, where everything is disposable, and objects are meant to be manipulated and benefit the individual. For Indigenous people, hope is our imagination. Our imagination benefits the collective and is interwoven into community. It takes imagination to make it through genocide. To survive boarding schools. To learn to make frybread. The tree might have been chopped all to hell, but our roots run deep. Our ancestors watered and replanted. Our imaginations give us permission to operate on our own terms. The sky's the limit. Our imaginations are rooted in tradition and point toward the stars.

DR. LEE FRANCIS 4
*Laguna Pueblo, Chief Imagination Officer of
the Indigenous Imagination Workshop*

[S]howing people how to do just that—embrace your culture no matter where you live—is what *The Fancy Navajo* is all about.... It's an understanding that our culture doesn't just stay behind in our homelands; it comes along with us wherever we go. A big part of that is food recipes. Many Indigenous cultures didn't traditionally have writing systems. So, someone says their grandma would make bread without using any measurements, which means they never learned to make bread. And I say gently, "It's OK to use measurements now. No one is going to judge you." And I give people tools to learn things they may have missed growing up. I think that's the balance—the *hózhó*—I bring with *The Fancy Navajo*.

ALANA YAZZIE
Diné, Author and Creator of The Fancy Navajo

◄◄◆►►

ALANA YAZZIE (B. 1987, SHE/HER) is Diné and a member of the Navajo Nation. In 2014, she created the popular lifestyle and food blog, *The Fancy Navajo*, which grew into an influencer channel on social media. Yazzie shared her life as a contemporary Diné/Navajo woman living in Phoenix, Arizona, and inspired others to embrace their culture by sharing recipes, fashion, and gardening tips infused with cultural knowledge. While many would point to Yazzie's recipe for Blue Corn Cupcakes as their favorite, Yazzie says the recipe with the most website hits is for her Fancy Navajo Magic Bread, because it can be hard for some to admit they need a bread recipe if their mother or grandmother never used one. For this reason, Yazzie's greatest passion is developing innovative and approachable recipes that use Indigenous and Southwestern ingredients. Yazzie enjoys showcasing her Navajo lifestyle in modern and bright settings to highlight the continued presence and thriving of Indigenous peoples. She is the author of *The Modern Navajo Kitchen*.

Now, as a mother, I look back and realize how important it was for me to hear [my grandfather] tell me over and over again, "You're O'odham because you are mine," no matter how mixed or Chicana I am. My grandfather's generation carried all these stories and experiences about our families and people forward so my generation could know who we are.... Because we lost our lands, our people are scattered. Our future will be so beautifully mixed.... It's important [our kids] understand the incredible sacrifices their ancestors made for them. The stories I'm carrying now—it's my responsibility to ensure the next generations never have to search for who they are or wonder where they come from.

DR. AMRAH SALOMÓN J.
O'odham, Mexican, Writer, Artist, Activist, and Educator

DR. AMRAH SALOMÓN J. (B. 1978, SHE/HER) is a queer-bi chingona of O'odham, Mexican, and European ancestry. She is a writer, artist, activist, and educator. Dr. Salomón is an assistant professor of English at the University of California, Santa Barbara, and a founding member of the Center for Interdisciplinary Environmental Justice. She is the co-founder of the Rez Beats Indigenous youth performance project, and a former member of the O'odham Anti Border Collective and Indigenous Action Media Collective. Dr. Salomón has a Ph.D. in ethnic studies from the University of California. She is the 2024 to 2025 University of California Hellman Fellow, a position that will assist in the completion of her forthcoming book, *Confluences: Indigenous Fugitivity on the Border*. The work traces the collective memory and history of Dr. Salomón's family and the non-federally recognized O'odham and Yoeme community from the Yuma, Arizona, area against processes of United States-Mexico border violence.

Storytelling has been a way for our communities to survive and thrive since time immemorial. Sharing stories helps us heal and understand ourselves. They celebrate our vivacity and diversity as Indigenous peoples. They guide us, from our very creation, to build the futures we want to bring to fruition for future generations. Without stories, I would not be here. I would not be alive. They sing me who I am. They are proof of generations of care and guidance. We are never alone as long as we remember.

KINSALE DRAKE
Diné, Poet, Editor, Playwright

KINSALE DRAKE (B. 2000, SHE/THEY) is Diné and a citizen of the Navajo Nation. She is an award-winning poet, editor, and playwright whose debut collection, *The Sky Was Once a Dark Blanket* (University of Georgia Press, 2024), won the 2023 National Poetry Series Competition. Drake's work has appeared in *Poetry*, *Best New Poets*, *The Atlantic*, TIME, NPR, MTV, and elsewhere. From 2017 to 2018, Drake served as a National Student Poet, appointed by the Library of Congress and the President's Committee on the Arts and Humanities. They have performed at the Library of Congress and twice at Carnegie Hall. They narrated audiobooks by Indigenous authors. Drake is a 2022 graduate of Yale College with bachelor of arts degrees in English and ethnicity, race, and migration. She has served as a guest faculty member for the Emerging Diné Writers Institute at Navajo Technical University since 2022, and teaches across the nation about storytelling, mental health, and poetry. When Drake is not teaching, winning awards, or walking fashion runways, she devotes her time to NDN Girls Book Club, a glittery-pink, wildly-successful nonprofit she founded to promote Indigenous literature at all reading levels.

There are parts of our history that are painful, but they do not define us. We define ourselves by the world we collectively build for current and future generations. It is up to all of us to tell our stories. And not just the stories of the bad times— but of those that we celebrate. Those that show our resilience, our strength, and our contributions.

DEB HAALAND
Laguna Pueblo, Politician

DEB HAALAND (B. 1960, SHE/HER) is from the Turquoise Clan of the Laguna Pueblo. Her traditional name means Crusted Turquoise in the Keres language. As the Interior Secretary from 2021 to 2025, Haaland was the first Native American to lead a cabinet agency. Haaland served as a United States representative for New Mexico's First Congressional District from 2019 to 2021. Haaland and Sharice Davids (Ho-Chunk) were the first Native American women elected to the United States Congress. Haaland received a Bachelor of Arts in English from the University of New Mexico and a juris doctor in Indian law from the University of New Mexico School of Law.

Today, instead of being removed from a landscape to make way for a public park, we are being invited back to our ancestral homelands to help prepare them and plan for the resilient future. We are being asked to apply our traditional knowledge to both the natural and human-caused ecological challenges, drought, erosion, visitation, etcetera, that are growing. What could be a better avenue of restorative justice than giving tribes the opportunity to participate in the management of lands their ancestors were removed from?

CARLETON BOWEKATY
A:shiwi (Pueblo of Zuni), Conservationist, Tribal Advocate

CARLETON BOWEKATY (B. 1980, HE/HIM) is A:shiwi (Zuni) from the Sun and Child of Tobacco clans. He is the policy director for the Bears Ears Partnership, a conservation and education organization for the cultural and natural landscapes of the greater Bears Ears region in Utah. Bowekaty was elected to the Pueblo of Zuni Tribal Council in 2015 and made Lieutenant Governor in 2018. He is a United States Army veteran who received numerous commendations, including the Meritorious Service Medal, Army Commendation Medal, and the Iraq Campaign Medal. Bowekaty was a former co-chair of the Bears Ears Inter-Tribal Coalition. Bowekaty's work engages other tribal nations seeking similar connections to their own landscapes and protection efforts.

MIKAH CARLOS (B. 1993, SHE/HER) is Onk Akimel O'odham, Tohono O'odham, and Piipaash. She is a member of the Salt River Pima-Maricopa Indian Community. Carlos was elected to Salt River Pima-Maricopa Indian Community (SRP-MIC) tribal council in 2022. She describes her early childhood as being removed from her culture. She was able to reconnect in upper elementary when she returned home to her tribal community. There, Carlos was able to immerse herself in traditional dances and language courses, a stark difference from her experiences in public school. Embracing her tribal community as extended family, Mikah strives to be a role model for Native youth, a resource for policymakers, and promotes tribal engagement. Carlos' accomplishments include running and being crowned Miss Salt River (2017 to 2018), serving locally on the SRP-MIC Young River Peoples Council, and serving nationally on the Center for Native American Youth Advisory Board, as a board member for the National Indian Child Welfare Association, and as co-president for the National Congress of American Indians Youth Commission.

I was able to start learning more about our *himdag*, which roughly translates to "way of life" in O'odham. This is a main component of our culture, and it encompasses an array of things that are hard to translate into English. When you learn about the himdag and culture, you learn your connection to the community and [y]our extended families. I began to understand the role and purpose I had in the community and finally that piece that felt like I was missing started to fall into place. . . . We know that culture is prevention and when it is incorporated holistically into services and programming for youth, we see a reduction in risky behaviors because of the protective factors that are incorporated into our cultural practices.

MIKAH CARLOS
Onk Akimel O'odham, Tohono O'odham, and Piipaash,
Tribal Leader, Child and Family Advocate

Reconnecting the Sacred

◄◆►

Reconnecting with what is most sacred can help balance a world that is difficult to keep up with; what is sacred is different for everyone. The voices echoing from the next pages are from leaders moving their communities through the sacred work of rematriation, reparations, tribal communications, and scholarship.

The Spanish missionary era, the gold rush cataclysm, and gentrification projects had horrific impacts on the region's first peoples. These tribes have ancestral ties dating back to time immemorial, with oral histories originating from some of California's more famous landmarks, including Úytaahkoo (White Mountain), the Karuk name for Mt. Shasta in Northern California, among others. Today, California is home to more people of Native American/Alaska Native heritage than any other state. California's tribal nations are as diverse as the state's vast landscapes, and each voice shared here is a changemaker moving their community with an eye toward the next sacred generations.

The voices in this sequence highlight their sacred reconnections in beautiful, sometimes devastating, but always powerful ways. Fueled with her people's traditional stories of hope and resilience, a scholar in northern California defies what non-Native anthropologists have touted as fact for years. A queer poet and a triple-tenured professor live more than one hundred miles apart but find common ground in the ways they use words to communicate prayer for generational thrivance—the enduring strength, resilience, and flourishing of their communities. Finally, after more than a century of suppressive fear-mongering tactics, the sacred knowledge of fire medicine is being reawakened by tribal matriarchs.

[My dad's passing] reshaped me and connected me to all my Lang relatives. . . . My Karuk family made me feel so welcome in a moment of sadness. It was 2022, and being called back as an adult made me have a better appreciation and understanding of how powerful and important this connection is; if I had tried to connect as a kid, I'm not sure the impact would have been the same. My beautiful Lang family and Karuk community have embraced me and told me how much they love me and that I'm not any less Karuk for having grown up away from the culture. . . . Having worked so hard and accomplished what I have in my life means so much more now that I can share it and spread positivity with the next generation of Karuk children.

NAOMI LANG
Karuk, Olympian

⫷◆⫸

NAOMI LANG (B. 1978, SHE/HER) is an enrolled member of the Karuk Tribe of California. She has a white mother and Native father, whose struggles with alcoholism distanced him from Lang, and by extension, disconnected her from her Karuk identity. As an adult, Lang was ready to reconnect with her father, but just as that was to happen, she learned he had passed away. Her uncle stepped in to teach her about her heritage—taking her around the Karuk territory, introducing her to her relatives, and teaching her the Karuk language. Reconnecting with her roots added deeper meaning to the resilience and joy she cultivated while figure skating throughout her childhood. She was the first Native American female athlete to participate in the Winter Olympics in 2002, competing as a figure skater in Salt Lake City, Utah. With skating partner Peter Tchernyshev, Lang is a two-time Four Continents champion (2000 and 2002), and a five-time United States national champion (1999 to 2003). The pair made it to the World Championships several times: They placed eighth in 2000; ninth in 2002; and eighth in 2003.

It's okay to be scared and feel like you don't know what you're doing. It's where everyone starts on each new project, no matter how seasoned or accomplished or knowledgeable. "Imposter Syndrome," however, is the devil of white supremacy-misogyny-homophobia on your shoulder really trying to get you to do its bidding via self-doubt, self-censorship, and self-defeat. Remember that. And don't listen.

TOMMY PICO
Kumeyaay, Poet and Screenwriter

TOMMY "TEEBS" PICO (B. 1983, HE/HIM) is from the Viejas Indian Reservation of the Kumeyaay Nation in California. Pico is an award-winning poet who has written for hit TV shows, including FX's *Reservation Dogs* and Peacock's *Resident Alien* and *Crystal Lake*. Pico is the author of *IRL* (2016), winner of the 2017 Brooklyn Library Literary Prize; *Nature Poem* (2017), winner of a 2018 American Book Award; *Junk* (2018), finalist for the 2019 Lambda Literary Award; and *Feed* (2019), a New York Times Notable Book of 2020 and finalist for the 2021 Kingsley Tufts Poetry Award. He was the 2013 Lambda Literary poetry fellow; a 2017 poetry fellow with the NYSCA/NYFA New York Foundation for the Arts; awarded the 2017 Friends of Literature prize from the Poetry Foundation; received a 2018 Whiting Award; and was an Artist-in-Residence for Sundance's Native Lab in 2021. Additionally, Pico co-curated the reading series *Poets With Attitude*, co-hosted the podcasts *Food 4 Thot* and *Scream, Queen!*, was a poetry editor at *Catapult Magazine*, and a contributing editor at *Literary Hub*.

Puyáamangay *is an Acjachemen word that means "always, constantly, eternally, for good."* *This word helps me stay rooted and guides the work I do in community to protect our sacred lands, waters, and cultures. . . . Mother Earth will survive the current climate crisis brought about by colonialism, extractivism, and greed. Whether or not we humans survive is another story. But it's not just whether we survive. It's how we survive. I believe [it] will come down to water. When we have our last glass of water, will we share it? . . . My hope and prayer is that I live my life in such a way that supports future generations to act always in a manner that is constantly, eternally, for good. Puyáamangay.*

ANGELA MOONEY D'ARCY
Acjachemen, Founder and Executive Director of the Sacred Places Institute
for Indigenous Peoples

ANGELA MOONEY D'ARCY (B. 1975, SHE/HER) is a member of the Acjachemen Nation and the founder and executive director of the Sacred Places Institute for Indigenous Peoples, a California Indigenous-led organization that works to build the capacity of Native nations and Indigenous peoples to protect sacred lands, waters, and cultures. She co-founded and co-directed the United Coalition to Protect Panhe, a grassroots alliance of Acjachemen people dedicated to the protection of their sacred sites, and served on the board of the Blas Aguilar Adobe Museum and Acjachemen Cultural Center. Mooney D'Arcy champions movements to rematriate land to California's tribal nations and protect sacred places from development and environmental degradation. She describes colonization as a violent severing of relationships between humans, nonhumans, land, water, culture, language, food, story, and song. Decolonization is about healing those relationships, which Mooney D'Arcy says should be honored for sustaining life for millennia. She earned her bachelor's degree from Brown University and her juris doctorate with a concentration in critical race studies and focus on federal Indian law from the UCLA School of Law. She currently lives and works in unceded Tongva homelands, also known as Los Angeles, California.

We must dismantle and decolonize outdated structures and rebuild wisely to ensure true self-determination for future generations. This isn't just an aspiration, but an urgent necessity. We must reshape our reality decisively, or risk having nothing to pass on. Our path forward must honor the full spectrum of Native experiences, building an inclusive future for all Indigenous peoples. We must nurture our community relationships while guarding against cultural and land exploitation. This work is our dedication to our ancestors and a promise to do better for those who follow.

DR. JOELY PROUDFIT
Luiseño/Payómkawichum, Tongva, Scholar, Activist, and Storyteller

◀◆▶

DR. JOELY PROUDFIT (B. 1969, SHE/HER) is a Payómkawichum and Tongva scholar, activist, and storyteller. A tenured professor three times over within the California State University system, she is the director of the California Indian Culture and Sovereignty Center and the department chair of American Indian Studies at California State University, San Marcos. She co-founded the nonprofit, California Indian Education for All, and owns Native Media Strategies, LLC, and Naqmayam Communications, a public relations, marketing, and advertising agency. Dr. Proudfit is often consulted by Hollywood media, television, and film productions regarding their Native content. In 2016, President Barack Obama appointed her to the National Advisory Council on Indian Education. In 2021, Dr. Proudfit became the first Indigenous woman appointed to the California Commission on the Status of Women and Girls. In 2022, *Variety* magazine honored her as one of their Entertainment Educators of the Year, and she was the National Indian Education Association's 2024 Educator of the Year. She holds a master's degree and Ph.D. in political science, with a focus on public policy and American Indian studies, from Northern Arizona University.

Fire is a spirit. It can help us reclaim our cultural practices, including our relationship with the land. It's important to understand that if we want a healthy ecosystem, then fire must be part of the solution. Nature alone cannot take care of itself. Humans are supposed to be part of the whole cycle; we can't sit around and wait for lightning to set fires for us. When we use fire safely, as it's meant to be, everything is restored.

MARGO ROBBINS
Yurok, Co-founder and Executive Director of the Cultural Fire Management Council

MARGO ROBBINS (B. 1961, SHE/HER) comes from the traditional Yurok village of Morek and is an enrolled member of the Yurok Tribe of Northern California. She is the co-founder and executive director of the Cultural Fire Management Council, which facilitates traditional and culturally-centered burning practices on Yurok lands. She is also one of the key planners and organizers of the Cultural Burn Training Exchange that takes place on the Yurok reservation twice a year. Robbins said for cultural lifeways to continue, people need to understand how vital fire is; traditional burning practices create a regenerative environment for plants, waterways, and wildlife to thrive after a fire. Robbins spent several years of her life as a water protector but said working to restore cultural fire practices is her life's calling; after being outlawed for more than one hundred years, the Yurok and other tribal nations have reclaimed the right to prescribe burns and are sharing fire knowledge with communities across the country. Robbins is a proud mother and grandmother who gathers and prepares traditional food and medicine, as well as a basket weaver and regalia maker. Robbins has served as co-lead of the Indigenous People's Burn Network, and a board member for the Indigenous Stewardship Network.

DR. CUTCHA RISLING BALDY (B. 1979, SHE/HER) is Hupa, Yurok, and Karuk and an enrolled member of the Hoopa Valley Tribe in Northern California. She is an associate professor of Native American Studies and the graduate program coordinator for the Master of Social Science in Environment and Community at California State Polytechnic University, Humboldt. Dr. Risling Baldy wrote *We Are Dancing For You* (2018), which uses a framework of Native feminisms to locate revitalization within a broad context of decolonizing praxis and considers how this renaissance of women's coming-of-age ceremonies confounds ethnographic depictions of Native women, challenges anthropological theories about menstruation, gender, and coming-of-age, and addresses gender inequality and gender violence within Native communities. In 2019, the book was named the Best First Book in Native American and Indigenous Studies award at the Native American Indigenous Studies Association Conference. She received her Ph.D. in Native American studies with a designated emphasis in feminist theory and research from the University of California, Davis, a master of fine arts degree from San Diego State University, and a bachelor's degree in psychology from Stanford University.

We are older than settler colonialism, our memories, our epigenetic markers, our DNA knows before settler colonialism, and it will know after settler colonialism. It will be here in the next world. For me, our history is not the history of the attempted or ongoing genocide of us. It is a history of survival, resistance, resurgence, and re-Indigenization. This is why my work centers our resurgence, our revitalization. Yes, it is important to understand the many nuances of this attempted genocide, but I also want to talk about us in complex ways that acknowledge we are more than what settlers wrote about us in archives, more than the documentation of our death.

DR. CUTCHA RISLING BALDY
Hupa, Yurok, Karuk, Author and Scholar

There was never a moment for me where I wasn't making art. The creating and the making and the concepts behind all of it—that's always been a Native thing. Our baskets, regalia, food—everything had meaning and purpose and story. . . . Making helps us understand ourselves. For me, in moments of trauma, creating art is my way to let my mind go idle or focus on something that's not the tragedy. Art heals. And it's not that I'm putting the tragedy into the art, but I'm creating to transform those feelings into something better and more powerful. Every piece of art I make is a better version of myself going out into the world, and I get a sense of peace from that.

JACOB A. MEDERS
Mechoopda, Maidu, Master Printmaker, Artist, and Educator

◄◆►

JACOB A. MEDERS (B. 1977, HE/HIM) is Mechoopda and Maidu and a member of the Mechoopda Indian Tribe of Chico Rancheria, California. Meders is a master printmaker and renowned artist, and he is an associate professor in the New College of Interdisciplinary Arts and Science at Arizona State University. In 2011, Meders established WarBird Press, a fine art printmaking studio. Meders has exhibited at the Museum of Contemporary Native Arts, the Jackie Headley Art Gallery, the Janet Turner Print Museum, the Heard Museum, the Wheelwright Museum, Museum Volkenkunde (Netherlands), the University of London, and the BACA Contemporary Native Art Biennial in Québec, Canada, among many other spaces. Meders's work focuses on altered perceptions of place, culture, and identity built on the assimilation and homogenization of Indigenous peoples. This work often ties into current issues faced in Indigenous communities. Meders earned his bachelor's degree in painting with a minor in printmaking from Savannah College of Art and Design and a master of fine arts in printmaking from Arizona State University.

Beyond Borders

When viewed from above at just the right angle and with a hint of squint, North and Central America form into the shape of a turtle, which is why many Indigenous nations in these regions refer to it as Turtle Island. Many nations have oral histories about a worldwide flood where humanity is saved by a large turtle that brings up land on her back, where life continues today. In none of these stories do borders exist.

Borders, like gender and race, are colonial fictions that create political divisions that benefit those in power and keep the oppressed severed. Borders are tools of violence and erasure that disrupt families, communities, culture, and wildlife. As sovereign nations, tribal citizens have the fundamental right to move within their own territory. For instance, in southern Arizona, the Tohono O'odham Nation includes sixty-two miles of international border; more than two thousand members reside in Mexico, and families often cross back and forth. In upstate New York, the Mohawk Nation at Akwesasne spans the United States-Canada border, known as the medicine line for offering Native war leaders refuge from colonizing armies once they crossed into Canada.

Colonial powers seek to separate Indigenous communities not just from their lands and cultures, but from each other—their communities and neighbors. Sovereignty requires that we honor our ancestral lands, languages, and memories, but it also demands we mend the wounds of settler colonialism by building up each other's communities in solidarity and in good relations. The voices in this sequence represent Indigenous nations that are separated by a division of some kind, but they all remind us of the powerful ways we remain connected beyond borders. This final segment connects voices from Alaska, Hawai'i, Pacific Islands and Polynesia, Mexico, and Canada breaking barriers in modeling, gender justice education, entertainment, grief, erotica, traditional skin marking and tattoo practices, social media, makeup, birthwork, music, ethnobotany, and ghost tours.

ARTIST Lehuauakea, *Mana Māhū*, Native Hawaiian

I want to pass on a legacy of healing, one that's restorative and restful; we are better when we take care of ourselves. Yeah, it's badass to get out there to slay and hustle, but there's so much power in the simple act of being restful. And, as anyone who does community work will tell you, being restful isn't simple. I give credit to Black femme folks for outlining strategies for how to put rest into action, and I've learned that our healing is meant to be communal. Showing up and being accountable—for work and for rest—shouldn't happen in isolation.

DR. CHARLENE AQPIK APOK
Iñupiaq, Co-Director of Gender Justice and Healing at Native Movement

DR. CHARLENE AQPIK APOK (B. 1984, SHE/THEY/ILAA) is Iñupiaq; her family is from White Mountain and Golovin, Alaska. She advocates for Indigenous rights to health and wellbeing, Indigenous sovereignty, and reclamation and creation of ceremony for all genders. Dr. Apok is the co-director of Gender Justice and Healing at Native Movement, an Indigenous-led nonprofit in Alaska; they are also the founding executive director of Data for Indigenous Justice, which homes data for Alaska for Missing and Murdered Indigenous relatives; and she is the co-founder of the Alaska Native Birthworkers Community, a collective of Indigenous birthworkers who provide Native families with free assistance for pregnancy, birth, postpartum care, and pregnancy loss. Dr. Apok earned a bachelor's degree in American ethnic studies, gender, women, and sexuality studies from the University of Washington, and a master's degree in Alaska Native studies and rural development and a Ph.D. in Indigenous studies from the University of Alaska Fairbanks.

I always say my songs come from those who walked before me. . . . I don't claim these songs. These sounds don't come from me. They come from the joy and spirit of my ancestors. I see the flute and the sounds we make as an extension of who we are, [as a way] to let our ancestors know we're listening, to let everyone else know we're still here. If these songs can help a lost one find their way back home or through the challenges of their community, then that's the legacy of this work.

MARY YOUNGBLOOD
Chugach Alutiiq, Cherokee, Seminole, Flutist

MARY YOUNGBLOOD (B. 1958, SHE/HER) is Chugach Alutiiq, Cherokee, and Seminole. Youngblood was adopted at a young age and is a survivor of the Indian boarding school era. Music helped her feel connected in a world that often made her feel like she didn't belong. Youngblood would become a world-renowned flutist and the first Native American woman to receive a Grammy Award for Best Native American Music Album and the first Native American to win two Grammy awards. She has won three Native American Music Awards, was the first female artist to win Flutist of the Year in 1999, won in the same category in 2000, and won Best Female Artist in 2000. The Library of Congress maintains eight of Youngblood's sound recordings. Her Grammy-nominated song, "Feed the Fire," was dedicated to all the women in her life, including her birth mother. The song is meant to evoke a feeling of dancing with the wind. She reflected on how life's winds can be unpredictable, carrying you in unexpected directions, but, much like a flute player's breath, they can also guide you home.

Outwardly what I do is storytelling, but for myself I call it channeling. It brings people together. We start out as strangers, and in ninety minutes, we're connected through this deep, personal experience of telling ghost stories. Western ideology might consider what I do as possessive or negative, but my people call it *Noho*, when an ancestor comes and sits on your shoulder to speak to you. Spiritual communication and connection is healing. It helps people look inside and begin their own journeys of healing.

LOPAKA KAPANUI
Kānaka Maoli/Native Hawaiian, Master Storyteller

◀◆▶

LOPAKA KAPANUI (1962, HE/HIM) is Kānaka Maoli, a Native Hawaiian master storyteller, author, actor, kumu hula, cultural practitioner, and former professional wrestler. Family legends, history, customs, and protocol were passed down to Kapanui in the traditional Hawaiian way, through *moʻolelo*, from mouth to ear, sitting at the feet of his mother and aunty; they would say *e mau ana ka ʻike* ("the knowledge must continue") at the end of each lesson. Sharing this knowledge is a gift and responsibility, Kapanui said. It was around the turn of the century that Kapanui, a spiritual medium his entire life, decided to capitalize on his storytelling talents and share his knowledge of paranormal histories through Mysteries of Hawaiʻi, the only Native Hawaiian-owned and operated ghost tour company in the state. Kapanui promises his tours are done with respect to patrons, the sites being visited, and the spirits communicating through him. Mysteries of Hawaiʻi refuses to use scare tactics or create hype where none exists. For his work, Lopaka was honored by the Hawaii State Legislature in 2020 for perpetuating the Hawaiian art of moʻolelo.

We need one another, and we owe our love, intention, care, protection, and presence to each other, the land, and our natural resources. This belief is ancestral, as it encompasses the protection of all that is sacred—land, water, and community—because what is sacred also nourishes and heals us. Grief work isn't solely about addressing the intense emotions that accompany loss; it also creates space for greater love, joy, and healing. This work equips individuals with tools and practices so they can consistently show up for self, loved ones, and community. We are dedicated to protecting the sacred, because the sacred protects us, too.

YVONNE MAHELONA
Native Hawaiian, Traditional Kanaka 'Oiwi Birth Worker, Grief Worker

YVONNE MAHELONA (B. 1989, SHE/HER) is Native Hawaiian and a traditional Kanaka 'Oiwi birth worker and grief worker. Mahelona said grief extends beyond death, such as in cases of incarceration, substance use, gentrification, development, or disasters, and even the absence of personal safety or resources. Mahelona is a student of *'oli*, traditional Hawaiian ceremony and chanting. Mahelona is also a fierce land and water protector and an anti-imperialist feminist community organizer with AF3IRM Hawai'i. Originally from Nanakuli Hawaiian Homestead on the island of O'ahu, Mahelona was raised by her great-grandmother. Her previous work includes research and advocacy for Missing and Murdered Native Hawaiian Women, Girls, and Mahu, as well as frontline organizing on Mauna Kea, the sacred mountain where she spent six months in 2019 with her people to block construction of the Thirty Meter Telescope. Answering the call of her *kūpuna* (community) and to honor Haumea, the goddess of childbirth and politics, Mahelona holds free grief circles, offers doula support to those who experience abortion and miscarriage, and educates about/advocates for reproductive justice.

MONTSERRAT "MONTSE" OLMOS LOZANO (B. 1991, ELLA/SHE) is Nahuatl, Chichimeca, Totonaca, and Mestiza. She is a traditional birth worker by ancestral inheritance and formally trained by Ancient Song Doula Services; she focuses on fertility, abortion, and postpartum care for queer, trans, Black, and Indigenous peoples of color. Olmos is the creator of Cultural Appropriation in Rebozo Work, the first-of-its-kind online course addressing the decolonial history of this sacred textile and its connection to anti-racism education. Ella is an international speaker on Indigenous sovereignty and autonomy, including issues related to extraction, the commodification of Indigenous knowledge and traditions, and racism within the birth community. Based in Mexico, Olmos provides abortion support, doula mentorship, and educational resources to birthing people. Olmos also cultivates corn, beans, squash, and medicinal herbs, is a performer of Son Jarocho and Son de Tarima, as well as a ceremonial dancer of Danza Conchera. Olmos was born in Mexico, grew up in the states of Nuevo León and Tamaulipas, and is a third-generation migrant across state and national colonial borders.

Agriculture and birthwork are about tending to life and cultivating life and caring for life. Often, that means we are trusting the unseen. When you put a seed in the ground, you don't get to see the process life undertakes; you must trust the seed knows what to do, that the roots will spread, the seed will grow, and soon you'll see a sprout. It's the same with midwifery and birthwork. We don't necessarily see what is happening inside, but we are trusting that the baby is going to grow and thrive.

MONTSERRAT "MONTSE" OLMOS LOZANO
Nahuatl, Chichimeca, Totonaca, and Mestiza, Traditional Birth Worker

Indigenous people were ready to embrace sex and erotica in a positive way. I think we were all quite exhausted with feeling like we had to frame our sexuality within the confines of trauma and violence and MMIW. Yes, those are important issues to address, but not all that shockingly, Indigenous people want desire and pleasure to be joyful and fun and erotic. I try to approach that in my work with humor and an open mind and an open heart. Whether I'm writing poetry or taking photographs, this is a safe, non–judgey, and ongoing conversation between me and Indigenous peoples from other communities who are looking to express their beautiful and vibrant sexualities.

TENILLE K. CAMPBELL
Dene, Métis, Poet, Photographer, and Scholar

TENILLE K. CAMPBELL (B. 1984, SHE/HER) is a Dene and Métis from English River First Nation in Saskatchewan, Canada. She is an award-winning writer and photographer whose debut poetry collection, *#IndianLovePoems* (2017), gained international attention for centering and reclaiming Indigenous erotica, humor, and spicy relationships. This was followed by *nedí nezy̨* (*Good Medicine*) (2021), another poetry collection. She won multiple Saskatchewan Book Awards and spent a year (2022 to 2023) serving as the Indigenous Joys residency lead artist with the Sâkêwêwak First Nations Artists' Collective in Regina. In 2024, Campbell was named the University of Saskatchewan's Indigenous Storyteller-in-Residence. She is the owner of sweetmoon photography and is known for documenting loving, vibrant, and contemporary Indigenous lifestyles. Campbell completed her master of fine arts degree in creative writing from the University of British Columbia and is working toward her Ph.D. at the University of Saskatchewan.

Our traditional tattooing practices went to sleep around the time of [colonial] contact for our communities. It has been a humble experience to help the tradition wake back up. The impacts of colonization have had rippling waves through the collective Indigenous experience. Our art, language, and our culture are the life raft our elders and ancestors ensured we would have. They went through generations of trauma and kept close the gifts and memory of our identity. It is our responsibility to know who we are, and to be proud and visible in a world where colonization is still prevalent. We have been who we have always been since time immemorial.

NAKKITA TRIMBLE-WILSON
Nisga'a, Traditional Tattoo Artist and Educator

NAKKITA TRIMBLE-WILSON (B. 1987, SHE/HER) is from the Nisga'a Nation in British Columbia, Canada. Trimble-Wilson, whose Nisga'a name is Algaxhl Gwilksk'alt'amtkw (Speaking Through Art), began practicing tattoo art in 2014; she is the only traditional tattoo artist in her community. Along with Nisga'a elders, Trimble-Wilson hopes to revive gihlee'e, the traditional process of tattooing, and reclaim Nisga'a ancestral tattooing methods of skin stitching and hand poking. Trimble-Wilson's work has been part of several exhibitions: at the Nisga'a Museum in British Columbia in 2014; in APTN's 2018 series, *Skindigenous*; and in the five-year traveling exhibit *Body Language: Reawakening Cultural Tattooing of the Northwest*. A practicing artist since 2007, Trimble-Wilson obtained her Master of Fine Arts degree from Emily Carr University in 2020. She is also an alumna of the Freda Diesing Program and completed her undergraduate degree at Alberta University of the Arts in Calgary. In 2018, Trimble-Wilson won the BC First Nations Art Fulmer Award, which recognizes artists for excellence in their craft.

I don't believe that we are supposed to stay within these colonial territories that were forced upon us. We were people of the seasons, and we were not static. I like to think of weather systems when I imagine how we used to move and break off into smaller bands and travel with the winds across the continent to network and trade. And now that all of this land has been stolen and commodified, I support all Natives who are standing strong wherever they are.

SIKOWIS NOBISS
Nêhiyaw, Saulteaux, Founder and Executive Director of the Great Plains Action Society

◄◄◆►►

SIKOWIS NOBISS (AKA, CHRISTINE NOBISS, B. 1977, SHE/HER) is Nêhiyaw/Plains Cree and Saulteaux/Ojibwe and a citizen of the George Gordon First Nation in Saskatchewan, Canada; she is also of Hungarian descent. Nobiss is the founder and executive director of the Great Plains Action Society (GPAS), a grassroots, Indigenous-led, climate and environment justice organization. In 2021, she received the Impact Through Advocacy award from the Iowa Environmental Council. GPAS received the OneIowa Community Partnership Award for its support of Two Spirit, trans, and LGBTQ+ justice work (2022) and was recognized for being a women-led organization doing excellent work in sustainability from the Johnson County United Nations Association Chapter (2023). Nobiss is a commissioner on the Iowa City Truth and Reconciliation Commission; she also sits on the Midwest Environmental Justice Grant Advisory Committee, the Centering Equity in the Sustainable Building Sector Governance Team, and the Just Transition Power Force as a guest expert working to reduce harmful practices in corporate procurement processes. Nobiss was nineteen when she held her first job with the New Brunswick Aboriginal Peoples Council in Fredericton, New Brunswick, Canada, during the Burnt Church Rebellion.

Everything about Cheekbone Beauty has truly been about digging deep into my Anishinaabe roots. Being sustainable and intentional about how we interact with all our relations, building community, living in a good way—Anishinaabe people have always done those things. And so, as I've been building Cheekbone, I'm constantly called to evolve how we do things, and that's innately Anishinaabe: adaptability. Today, for me, that looks like doing the hard work to build an actual science lab, hand-source natural ingredients—mica and shea butter, for instance. We meet with experts, we try different formulas, make sure it's sustainable, and go back to the drawing board if something isn't right....This work is literally my ancestral Anishinaabe knowledge screaming from my blood.

JENN HARPER
Ojibwe, Founder and CEO of Cheekbone Beauty Cosmetics Inc.

JENN HARPER (B. 1976, SHE/HER) is Ojibwe/Anishinaabe and registered with Northwest Angle #33 First Nation in Ontario, Canada. Harper is the founder and CEO of Cheekbone Beauty Cosmetics Inc., a household beauty brand sold online and in stores like Sephora across the United States and Canada—the first Indigenous-owned beauty brand of its kind. Harper's brand delivers high-quality, vegan, cruelty-free products designed for low environmental impact and maximum wearability. Harper has earned many recognitions: She was named one of the 2019 Women of the Year by *Chatelaine* Magazine; was listed as one of *Entrepreneur* Magazine's 100 Women of Influence in 2022; and in 2023, received an honorary doctorate from Brock University for her commitment to sustainability and commitment to her community. Since its inception, Cheekbone Beauty has given over $250,000 in monetary and in-kind donations to the First Nations Child and Family Caring Society, as well as initiatives advocating for clean drinking water, solar power, and tree planting for Indigenous communities.

DION KASZAS (B. 1977, HE/HIM) is a Nlaka'pamux, Métis, and Hungarian professional tattoo artist, Indigenous ancestral skin marker, transformative blackworker, and host of the *Transformative Marks* podcast. Kaszas has been a professional tattoo artist for more than fifteen years and works at the HFX Tattoo Company in Bedford, Nova Scotia. Kaszas is a leader for his efforts to revitalize Indigenous tattoo practices in Canada; his work has been featured in *Beside* magazine, *The New York Times*, and *The World Atlas of Tattoo* (2015). Kaszas was featured in the *APTN* documentary series *Skindigenous*, the *Fox Nation* series *USA INK*, and the multi-award-winning documentary film *This Ink Runs Deep* (2019). Kaszas specializes in large blackwork and tribal tattoo designs and his practice seeks to minimize shame, guilt, or inadequacy surrounding tattoos and one's reasons for having work done. He said it's easy to romanticize traditional tattoo designs and their meanings, but argued that his ancestors, like today's relatives, marked themselves for many reasons, including connecting with dreams or spirits, for healing or prayer, for identification, and for beautification and adornment.

Many of the goals that I had when I started this work are coming true today: Our young people are growing up with ancestral skin marking practices and will not know a world where our people didn't mark themselves. We now have a generation growing up and assuming that tattoo gatherings, medicine markings, coming-of-age marks, and facial marks are just part of our cultures, and this is just what we do. I envision a future where each community has an ancestral skin marker or two. I hope this practice is never silenced again—that each dot, each stitch, and each line will continue to make our community members, families, nations, the earth, and all that is whole again.

DION KASZAS
Nlaka'pamux, Métis, Tattoo artist, Indigenous Ancestral Skin Marker, and Transformative Blackworker

> Our treaties stand the test of time. They are the Supreme Law of this land. If a nation's honor and exceptionalism is a measure of its integrity to its own laws and creed, then one must look no further than the United States' continued abrogation of its own treaties to recognize that its honor is in short supply.

WILLIAM "BILL" SMITH

Eyak, National Indian Health Board Chair, Vice President of the Valdez (Alaska) Native Tribe Board of Directors, United States Army Veteran

WILLIAM "BILL" SMITH (B. 1952, HE/HIM) is Eyak and a member of the Valdez Native Tribe of Alaska. He is the son of Chief Marie Smith-Jones, the last full-blooded speaker of the Eyak language. His father was a fisherman. Smith is vice president of the Valdez Native Tribe's Board of Directors and is the chairman of the National Indian Health Board. Smith enlisted with the United States Army at seventeen as a heavy-duty mechanic and a recovery specialist. He toured Augsburg, Germany with the 1/36 field artillery, then toured Long Bình Vietnam from 1971 to 1972. He returned to the state—Fort Huachuca, Arizona—but shipped back to Germany with the 5/68 armor tank outfit. Smith retired from service in 1977 and returned to Alaska. He serves on the Alaska Native Health Board and is one of the local tribal veterans representatives. Smith is a fierce advocate for Indigenous issues and educates lawmakers about their federal responsibilities to the wellbeing of Indigenous peoples across the country.

The state of Alaska needs a major shift in its policies and approaches to working with Alaska Native tribes and people. We are not an enemy of the state. This is our home, and we love it. But we need to be respected and honored as equals. . . . Let us enter into a new era of equality and real trust and responsibility. Please stop fighting our peoples' basic human rights to provide for the survival and wellbeing of our people.

EVON PETER
Neets'aii Gwich'in, Koyukon Athabascan, Indigenous Language, Rights, and Knowledge Advocate

EVON PETER (B. 1975, HE/HIM) is Neets'aii Gwich'in from Vashrąįį K'ǫǫ (Arctic Village), Alaska. He is a senior research scientist at the Center for Alaska Native Health Research at the University of Alaska Fairbanks (UAF). In 1999, at age twenty-four, Peter became the youngest person ever elected Chief of Vashrąįį K'ǫǫ. In 2014, Peter was appointed vice chancellor for Rural, Community, and Native Education at UAF. He was responsible for managing six community campuses across the state and serving students who spoke fourteen Indigenous languages and represented 140 tribal governments. In 2021, Peter pivoted from academia back to community-based language revitalization and suicide prevention with the intention of creating a Dinjii Zhuh K'yàa (Gwich'in language) immersion school, a passion that continues today. He serves as a board member of the Gwich'in Council International and the Gwich'in Social and Cultural Institute of Alaska. Peter has a bachelor's degree in Alaska Native studies and a master's degree in rural development, both from UAF.

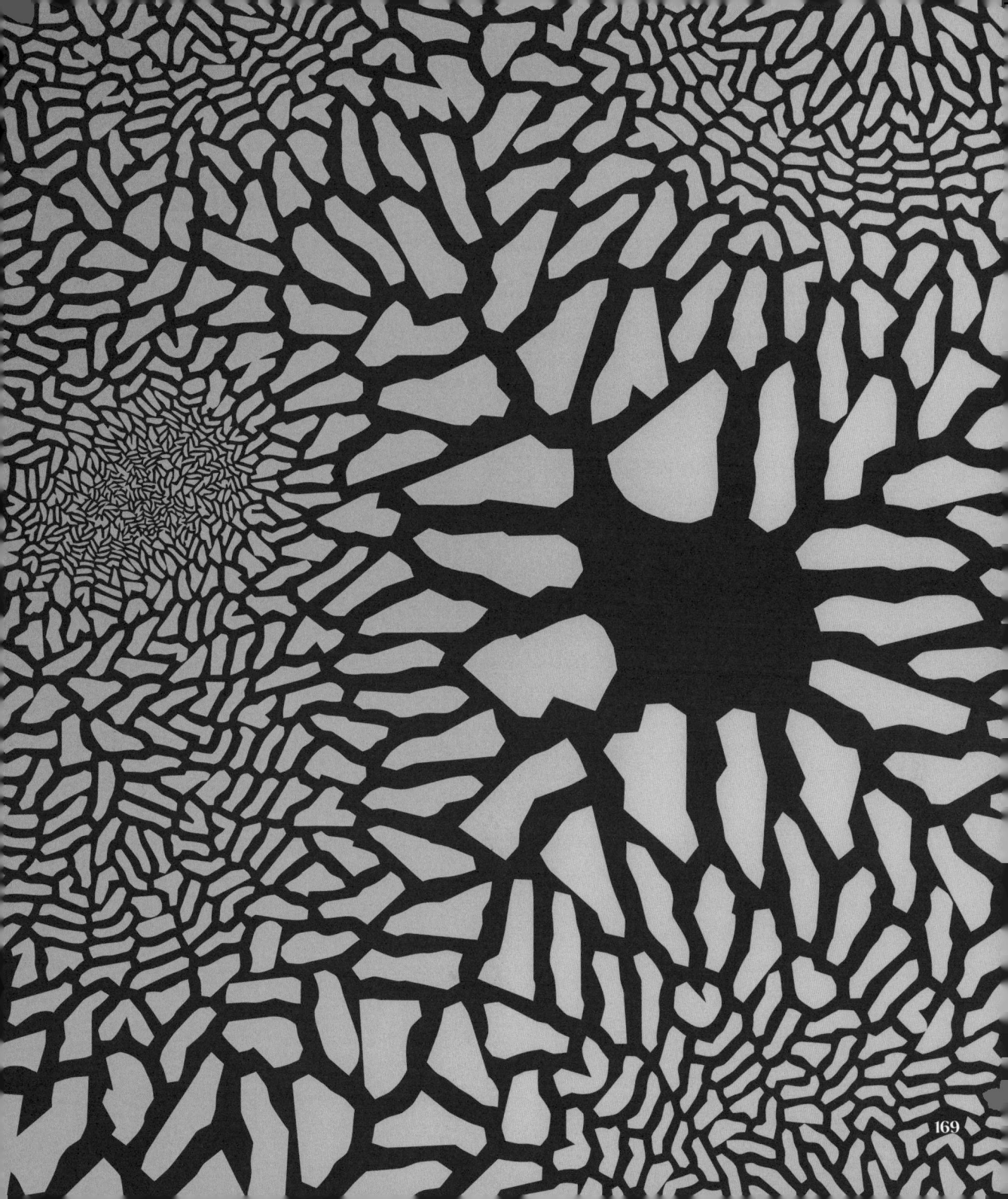

Prior to contact with Europeans, tribal child-rearing practices and beliefs allowed a natural system of child protection to flourish. Traditional Indian spiritual beliefs reinforced that all things had a spiritual nature that demanded respect, including children. Not only were children respected, but they were also taught to respect others. Extraordinary patience and tolerance marked the methods that were used to teach Indian children self-discipline. At the heart of this natural system of beliefs, traditions, and customs, was an interdependent network of extended family community, all of which share child-rearing responsibilities. In this way, the protection of children in the tribe was the responsibility of all people in the community.

DR. SARAH KASTELIC
Alutiiq, Child and Family Welfare Advocate

DR. SARAH KASTELIC (B. 1974, SHE/HER) is Alutiiq and an enrolled citizen of the Alaska Native Village of Ouzinkie. Dr. Kastelic became the executive director of the National Indian Child Welfare Association (NICWA) in January 2015. Prior to joining NICWA as chief of staff in 2011, she led the National Congress of American Indians' welfare reform program and, in 2003, was the founding director of the National Congress of American Indians (NCAI) Policy Research Center. She began her career at the Bureau of Indian Affairs central office as a child welfare specialist in 1998. She earned a master's degree and Ph.D. from the Brown School of Social Work at Washington University in St. Louis, where she serves as adjunct faculty. Dr. Kastelic has served as a principal investigator of several national, federally and privately funded research projects, partnering with tribal and urban Indian communities.

We live in relationship with ourselves, with each other, and with place and land. These relationships inform our identities. Teaching and learning is inherently connected to relationship and identity. To ignore this is to think only of teaching as a transaction of information. It is, however, much more than that. Teaching and learning is about coming to understand ourselves, each other, and this earth more fully.

JO CHRONA
Ts'msyen/Tsimshian, Two Spirit Educator, Advocate, and Author

◀◆▶

JO CHRONA (B. 1965, SHE/HER) is Ts'msyen/Tsimshian and is Ganhada (Raven) of Waap (House) K'oom of the Kitsumkalum First Nation; she is also of European heritage. Chrona is a Two Spirit speaker, education consultant, Indigenous education advocate, and author of *Wayi Wah! Indigenous Pedagogies: An Act for Reconciliation and Anti-Racist Education* (2022). Chrona is passionate about creating systemic change to build inclusive, strength-based education experiences for all learners. Chrona is a certified teacher with a master's degree in educational technology from the University of British Columbia and decades of experience in K to 12 and post-secondary systems. She has been instrumental in assisting the transformation of British Columbia's education systems in a variety of roles, including working with a First Nations-led education advocacy organization and as an advisor to the British Columbia Ministry of Education; she has worked on curriculum and professional development, resource writing, and Indigenous education. Chrona has continued to provide professional learning workshops on Indigenous education and anti-racism. Chrona earned her undergraduate degree from Simon Fraser University and completed UBC's Transformative Educational Leadership Program.

Index of Individuals

Featured Indigenous Nations

Everyday Warriors

STANDING ROCK SIOUX TRIBE

The Standing Rock Sioux Tribe has sixteen thousand enrolled citizens and spans 2.3 million acres of prairie bordering the Missouri River in North and South Dakota. It was the site of the Dakota Access Pipeline protests.

PINE RIDGE INDIAN RESERVATION

The Pine Ridge Indian Reservation is home to the Oglala Sioux Tribe, which boasts a membership of about fifty-two thousand enrollees. This thrity-five-hundred-square-mile reservation in southwestern South Dakota includes Wounded Knee, where three hundred Lakota were massacred in 1890.

CHEYENNE RIVER SIOUX TRIBE OF SOUTH DAKOTA

The Cheyenne River Sioux Tribe has sixteen thousand citizens, with 70 percent living on 1.6 million acres in central South Dakota. Its tribal government has banned hostile lawmakers from entering sovereign lands.

RED LAKE BAND OF CHIPPEWA INDIANS

The Red Lake Reservation spans thirteen hundred square miles in northwest Minnesota and has seventeen thousand members. The tribe is known for wild rice harvesting and walleye fishing.

THREE AFFILIATED TRIBES

The Mandan, Hidatsa, and Arikara Nation, also called the Three Affiliated Tribes, resides on the 988,000-acre Fort Berthold Indian Reservation in central North Dakota on the Missouri River, with over seventeen members.

TURTLE MOUNTAIN BAND OF CHIPPEWA INDIANS

Located near the Canadian border in North Dakota, the Turtle Mountain Band of Chippewa Indians has thirty-three thousand members. In 2025, the tribe welcomed home its most famous member Leonard Peltier after he was granted clemency.

CROW RESERVATION IN MONTANA

The Crow Indian Reservation covers 2.2 million acres and has eleven thousand members, 85 percent of whom speak Crow as their first language. Many members prefer Apsáalooke (children of the large-beaked bird) to Crow.

FT. PECK TRIBES IN MONTANA

The Fort Peck Reservation is home to the Oceti Sakowin (Sioux) bands, including the Sisseton/Wahpeton, Yanktonai, and Teton Hunkpapa, as well as the Assiniboine bands of Canoe Paddler and Red Bottom. Fort Peck has about twelve thousand enrolled members, spanning more than two million acres in northeastern Montana.

NORTHERN CHEYENNE TRIBE OF MONTANA

The Northern Cheyenne Reservation in Montana covers 440,000 acres and has more than eleven thousand members. The tribe call themselves Tsis tsis'tas (the beautiful people). Their annual Fort Robinson Spiritual Run honors ancestors' escape from captivity in 1879.

WINNEBAGO TRIBE OF NEBRASKA

The Winnebago Tribe is in northeastern Nebraska, near the Iowa border. Its reservation is about 27,600 acres, with five thousand members who call themselves Ho-Chunk and ties to several Native celebrities, from Lillian St. Cyr, aka Red Wing to Joba Chamberlain.

OMAHA TRIBE OF NEBRASKA

The Omaha Tribe of Nebraska has around five thousand enrolled members, three thousand of whom live on a 310-square-mile reservation in Macy, Nebraska. The tribe is credited by non-Native "experts" for being the first on the Northern Plains to adopt equestrian culture around 1770.

IOWA TRIBE OF KANSAS AND NEBRASKA

This tribe has forty-three hundred enrolled members. The reservation is located in southeastern Nebraska/northeastern Kansas and spans fifteen hundred acres of checkerboard lands, alternating between tribal and non-Native ownership.

PAWNEE NATION OF OKLAHOMA

The Pawnee Nation of Oklahoma has about thirty-five thousand enrolled members. The Pawnee Nation's jurisdictional area covers approximately sixty thousand acres plus seventy-six thousand mineral acres.

KIOWA TRIBE OF OKLAHOMA

There are about 10,600 enrolled citizens of the Kiowa Tribe of Oklahoma. The 1867 Medicine Lodge Treaty established the 2.8-million-acre Kiowa-Comanche-Apache Reservation. The Kiowa share their reservation lands with the Comanche between the Washita and Red rivers, centering on Anadarko, Oklahoma.

Stories and Tellers

JAMESTOWN S'KLALLAM TRIBE

The Jamestown S'Klallam Tribe, based on Washington's Northern Olympic Peninsula, has over five hundred members. Their reservation spans 13.49 acres, with an additional one thousand plus acres of traditional and sacred sites. Since 1989, they've produced over forty watershed plans, studies, and recovery initiatives.

LUMMI NATION

Lummi Nation, Washington's third-largest tribe, has over five thousand members and a thirteen thousand-acre reservation near the Medicine Line (Canadian border). Canoes are central to Lummi culture.

MAKAH TRIBE OF NEAH BAY, WASHINGTON

The Makah Reservation is forty-seven square miles located at the most northwest point of the continental United States. The tribe has about fourteen hundred enrolled members. The name "Makah" means "people generous with food" in Salish.

NISQUALLY INDIAN TRIBE

The Nisqually Tribe is located east of Olympia, Washington and has about nine hundred enrolled members. The Nisqually Indian Reservation covers about five thousand acres; tribal land holdings, on and near the Nisqually reservation, exceed one thousand acres.

SPOKANE NATION IN WASHINGTON

The Spokane Tribe of Indians, with two thousand members, resides on a 159,000-acre reservation in eastern Washington. Federal legislation in 2020 compensated the tribe for twenty-five hundred acres lost to the Grand Coulee Dam.

TULALIP TRIBES OF WASHINGTON

The Tulalip Tribes, located north of Seattle, have four thousand members, spanning a twenty-two-thousand-acre reservation. In 2025, Tulalip secured a landmark data sharing agreement with the Washington State Department of Health to promote tribal data sovereignty.

QUINAULT INDIAN NATION IN WASHINGTON

The Quinault Nation, with over three thousand members, has a two hundred-thousand-acre reservation located at the southwest corner of the Olympic Peninsula.

CONFEDERATED TRIBES AND BANDS OF THE YAKAMA NATION

The Yakama Nation, located in southern Washington, has eleven thousand members and a 1.3-million-acre reservation, home to one of the nation's largest commercial forests. The nation comprises of fourteen different bands.

CONFEDERATED TRIBES OF THE UMATILLA INDIAN RESERVATION IN OREGON

The Umatilla Indian Reservation in northeast Oregon spans 172,000 acres and has over thirty-two hundred members. The three tribes of the Confederation—the Umatilla, Walla Walla, and Cayuse—were renowned for their horsemanship.

CONFEDERATED TRIBES OF THE GRAND RONDE COMMUNITY OF OREGON

The Grand Ronde Community in Oregon, home to over thirty tribes and bands like the Kalapuya, Molalla, and Chinook, spans 11,500 acres. It is governed by a nine-member council and has about fifty-four hundred enrolled members.

CONFEDERATED TRIBES OF SILETZ INDIANS OF OREGON

The Tribes of Siletz Indians is a confederation of more than twenty-seven tribes and bands. The Confederated Tribes have fifty-six hundred enrolled members and span a thirty-nine hundred-acre reservation.

Roots and Relations

LITTLE RIVER BAND OF OTTAWA INDIANS OF MICHIGAN

The Little River Band of Ottawa Indians descends from the Grand River Ottawa Bands, historically living along the Manistee River, Pere Marquette River, and the Grand River system on some fifteen million acres. Federally reaffirmed in 1994, its reservation spans 540 acres with five thousand enrolled members.

SAGINAW CHIPPEWA TRIBE OF MICHIGAN

Located in central Michigan, Saginaw Chippewa Indian Tribe has about thirty-five hundred enrolled members and its reservation—known as Isabella Indian Reservation—covers 138,240 acres. In 1998, the tribe established Saginaw Chippewa Tribal College, an accredited two-year community college.

HO-CHUNK NATION OF WISCONSIN

The Ho-Chunk Nation is a "non-reservation" tribe, as members have had to purchase private land to regain title to ancestral territory. The Ho-Chunk were forcibly removed more than thirteen times; today, the Nation has about eight thousand enrolled citizens and a growing with lands totaling about ten thousand acres.

ONEIDA NATION IN WISCONSIN

The Oneida Reservation is laid out along the Fox River. There are more than seventeen thousand enrolled members. The Oneida Nation is one of the largest employers in northeastern Wisconsin with over three thousand employees.

SOKAOGON CHIPPEWA COMMUNITY MOLE LAKE BAND OF LAKE SUPERIOR CHIPPEWA IN WISCONSIN

The Sokaogon Chippewa Community has about 1,500 members and a nearly five thousand-acre Mole Lake Reservation. They are known as the "Lost Tribe" because their twelve-mile-square reservation title from the 1854 Treaty was lost in a Lake Superior shipwreck.

SHINNECOCK INDIAN NATION

The Shinnecock Indian Nation is headquartered in Southampton, New York and was federally recognized in 2010. Its tribal territory encompasses nine hundred acres at Shinnecock Neck, as well as one hundred acres along the Peconic Bay. There are about sixteen hundred enrolled members.

SEACONKE WAMPANOAG TRIBE

The Seaconke Wampanoag Tribe, with ancestral lands in Rhode Island and Massachusetts, is state-recognized in Massachusetts since 1997 but lacks federal recognition, reservation lands, and enrollment figures. Part of its five thousand members has unsuccessfully sought recognition in Rhode Island, facing opposition from the solo federally recognized Narragansett Tribe.

MOHEGAN TRIBE

The Mohegan Nation Land Claim Settlement Act of 1994 placed the cleaned-up United Nuclear site in Connecticut into trust as Mohegan reservation land. The tribe, with over twenty-three hundred members, has reclaimed ancestral land, totaling over five hundred acres.

PENOBSCOT NATION IN MAINE

The Penobscot Nation in Maine, with over twenty-four hundred members, holds forty-nine hundred acres of reservation land, including two hundred plus islands in the Penobscot River, and ninety thousand acres of trust land across the state. They will receive the largest land return in U.S. history—thirty-one thousand acres from the Trust for Public Land, a national nonprofit.

HALIWA-SAPONI INDIAN TRIBE

The Haliwa-Saponi Indian Tribe is a state-recognized in North Carolina with more than four thousand enrolled members, who are direct descendants of the Saponi, Tuscarora, Tutelo, and Nansemond people.

Innovators and Influencers

BORIKUA TAÍNO

Borikua Taíno are descendants of Puerto Rico's Indigenous peoples, including the Diaspora. While not formally recognized, over 110,000 claimed Taíno heritage in 2022 (U.S. Census). They work to preserve their culture and advocate for Indigenous rights and inclusion in Puerto Rican society.

SEMINOLE TRIBE OF FLORIDA

The Seminole Tribe of Florida controls over ninety thousand acres across six reservations in south Florida, with more than forty-two hundred members. In 1975, they pioneered tribal gaming with tax-free smoke shops and a high-stakes bingo operation.

CHEROKEE NATION

The Cherokee Nation, the largest U.S. tribe with over 450,000 citizens, has a seven thousand-square-mile reservation in northeastern Oklahoma. In 1838, the Cherokee were forcibly relocated via the "Trail of Tears," a thousand-mile journey that claimed nearly four thousand lives.

MUSCOGEE (CREEK) NATION IN OKLAHOMA

The Muscogee (Creek) Nation has about seventy thousand tribal members. As of 2020, the tribe's reservation boundaries include much of Tulsa and eastern Oklahoma after the United States Supreme Court ruled to uphold tribal sovereignty, tribal boundaries, and treaty obligations.

CHICKASAW NATION

The Chickasaw Nation's reservation spans more than seventy-six hundred square miles in south-central Oklahoma. The Chickasaw are the twelfth largest tribe in the United States with a population exceeding eighty thousand citizens.

CHEYENNE AND ARAPAHO TRIBES OF OKLAHOMA

The Cheyenne and Arapaho Tribes of Oklahoma, with over twelve thousand citizens, own over ten thousand acres and oversee seventy thousand acres of individual allotments. They allied in the eighteenth century and established a unified tribal government in 1937.

KICKAPOO NATION OF OKLAHOMA

The Kickapoo Tribe of Oklahoma has more than twenty-six hundred enrolled tribal members, with about two thousand residing within the state. The tribal jurisdictional area covers about one hundred thousand acres in central Oklahoma.

LIPAN APACHE TRIBE OF TEXAS

The Lipan Apache Tribe of Texas, a state-recognized nonprofit, has about forty-five hundred members. In 2021, Presidio officials transferred the Cementerio del Barrio de los Lipanes to the tribe, which collaborates with the Big Bend Conservation Alliance to protect and study the site.

Desert Heartwork

SALT RIVER PIMA-MARICOPA INDIAN COMMUNITY

The Salt River Pima-Maricopa Indian Community spans nearly fifty-three thousand acres along Arizona's Phoenix Valley and is home to over eleven thousand citizens from the Pima (O'odham) and Maricopa (Piipaash) tribes.

TOHONO O'ODHAM

Tohono O'odham, meaning "desert people," has about twenty-eight thousand citizens, primarily on nearly three million acres of tribal land in southern Arizona, the state's second-largest reservation. Nearby Mexico is home to some O'odham communities near the Nation's southern edge.

PASCUA YAQUI TRIBE OF TUCSON

The Pascua Yaqui Tribe has about twenty-one thousand citizens and twenty-two hundred acres of land in Southern Arizona. The Pascua Yaqui Tribe was federally recognized in 1978. Yaqui spirituality has a close connection to deer that includes the deer dancer society.

HOPI TRIBE

The Hopi Tribe has about 14,500 citizens. The tribe has nearly two million acres of land and is made up of twelve villages and three mesas in northeast Arizona. Hopi has one of the oldest villages in the country in Old Oraibi and Hopi land is surrounded by the Navajo Nation.

PUEBLO OF ZUNI

Zuni Pueblo has one of the largest populations of pueblos in New Mexico with more than ten thousand citizens. Zuni encompasses about four-hundred and fifty thousand acres in northwestern New Mexico.

NAVAJO NATION

The Navajo Nation has more than four hundred thousand citizens and has the largest landmass in the United States of any tribe in Arizona, New Mexico, and Utah. It covers more than twenty-seven thousand square miles and is larger than ten of the fifty states in the country.

PUEBLO OF LAGUNA

The Laguna Pueblo has six villages spread across its five-hundred thousand acres of land in west-central New Mexico. The Pueblo has about seventy-eight hundred citizens. Laguna translates to "small lake" in Spanish and derives from a lake on tribal land.

Reconnecting the Sacred

KARUK TRIBE OF CALIFORNIA

The Karuk Tribe, California's second-largest with around four thousand members and five thousand descendants, historically occupied over a million acres along the Klamath River. They now manage nine hundred acres of trust land and eight hundred acres of fee land.

VIEJAS INDIAN RESERVATION OF THE KUMEYAAY NATION IN CALIFORNIA

The Viejas Indian Reservation, spanning sixteen hundred acres in San Diego County, California, is home to the Viejas Band of Kumeyaay Indians, with about four hundred members. The Kumeyaay have a rich regional history dating back over ten thousand years.

ACJACHEMEN NATION

The Juaneño Band of Mission Indians, Acjachemen Nation, are the original inhabitants of what is now Orange County and parts of San Diego, Los Angeles, and Riverside counties. Despite state recognition and eighteen hundred members, they have fought unsuccessfully for federal recognition for over three decades.

PAYÓMKAWICHUM

Six federally recognized Luiseño (Payómkawichum) tribes in southern California—La Jolla, Pala, Pauma, Pechanga, Rincon, and Soboba—have reservations and a combined population of around six thousand, overseeing over sixty-five square miles. The San Luis Rey Band is not federally recognized.

TONGVA

The Tongva people have lived in the Greater Los Angeles Basin for thousands of years. Enslaved by Spanish colonizers in the late 1700s, they were forced to build the Misión de San Gabriel Arcángel, leading to the name "Gabrieleño." The state-recognized Gabrielino/Tongva Nation has over four thousand self-identified descendants.

YUROK TRIBE

The Yurok Tribe, California's largest with over 6,500 members, holds an eighty-five-square-mile reservation, forty-four miles of which span the Klamath River. In 2024, they partnered with the National Park Service to manage 125 acres of returned land and played a key role in the largest United States dam removal project.

HOOPA VALLEY TRIBE

The Hoopa Valley Tribe, with over twenty-five hundred members, holds more than 102,000 acres in Northern California. In 2023, they acquired ten thousand additional acres of Hupa Mountain property.

MECHOOPDA INDIAN TRIBE OF CHICO RANCHERIA, CALIFORNIA

The Mechoopda Indian Tribe of Chico Rancheria, with around six hundred members, lost its twenty-six-acre reservation during the mid-twentieth-century tribal termination era. Federally re-recognized in 1992, the tribe acquired over thirteen hundred acres within two decades.

Beyond Borders

IÑUPIAQ

The Iñupiat, or "the real people," are Alaska Natives with traditional lands in northern and northwestern Alaska. Nearly fourteen thousand Iñupiat live in over thirty Arctic villages, including Utqiaġvik, Wainwright, and Point Hope.

NATIVE VILLAGE OF PALUWIK (PORT GRAHAM), ALASKA

The Native Village of Paluwik, an Alutiiq community on the southern Kenai Peninsula is home to about three to four hundred Sugpiaq tribal members. It lies on the western shore of Port Graham Bay.

VALDEZ NATIVE TRIBE OF ALASKA

The Valdez Native Tribe, a 501(c)(3) nonprofit in Valdez, Alaska, serves the Native community with 205 base roll members, over 170 additional enrollees, and more than 430 eligible beneficiaries.

VASHRAJI K'OO (ARCTIC VILLAGE)

Vashraji K'oo, or "Arctic Village" in Gwich'in, is an unincorporated Native village in Yukon-Koyukuk Census Area, Alaska, with a stable population of about 150 over thirty years. Most residents speak and understand Gwich'in.

ALASKA NATIVE VILLAGE OF OUZINKIE

Ouzinkie, a rural village on Spruce Island north of Kodiak Island, is accessible only by boat or plane. Home to over 125 year-round residents, its Alutiiq people have lived in the region for thousands of years.

KĀNAKA MAOLI/NATIVE HAWAIIAN

Kānaka Maoli, a term used by Native Hawaiians to describe themselves, are not federally recognized as a tribe. They make up about 27 percent of Hawaii's 1.2 million population, residing in the 137 islands, reefs, and ledges of the Hawaiian Archipelago (Ka Pae Aina).

KITSUMKALUM FIRST NATION

The Kitsumkalum First Nation, a Tsimshian band in British Columbia, Canada, has about 900 members, with 250 living on reserve. Archaeological evidence traces their presence in the area to at least five thousand years ago.

ENGLISH RIVER FIRST NATION

The English River First Nation is a Dene Nation band government in Patuanak, Saskatchewan, Canada. Their reserve is in the northern section of the province. Its territories are in the boreal forest of the Canadian Shield. Tribal membership is roughly two thousand members.

NISGA'A NATION

The Nisga'a Nation, with about seven thousand members, resides in four villages and urban centers like Terrace and Prince Rupert in British Columbia. Original inhabitants of the Nass River Valley, they achieved self-government and land control through the landmark Nisga'a Final Agreement (1998-2000).

GEORGE GORDON FIRST NATION

The George Gordon First Nation, a Plains Cree and Saulteaux community in Touchwood Hills, Saskatchewan, signed Treaty 4 in 1874. With around four thousand members, over one thousand live on-reserve, speaking Cree, Saulteaux, and English.

NORTHWEST ANGLE #33 FIRST NATION IN ONTARIO, CANADA

Northwest Angle #33 First Nation, an Anishinaabe/Ojibwe band in Kenora District, Ontario, Canada, has two communities: Angle Inlet, accessible by water or air, and Dog Paw. The nation has over six hundred registered members.

NLAKA'PAMUX

The Nlaka'pamux Nation, with over six thousand people in fifteen bands across British Columbia's Thompson-Nicola region, is governed by the Nlaka'pamux Nation Tribal Council (NNTC). NNTC membership is Nlaka'pamux-based, not band-based, reflecting their self-governance and rights, independent of the Indian Act.

MÉTIS

The Métis Nation's historic homeland spans Canada's prairie provinces and parts of Ontario, British Columbia, the Northwest Territories, and the northern U.S. Of 700,000 Métis in Canada, 250,000 are enrolled members, making them one of three legally recognized Indigenous peoples alongside First Nations and Inuit.

TOTONACA

The Totonac are an Indigenous Mesoamerican people from east-central Mexico's Totonacapan region, spanning Gulf lowlands to the Sierra Norte de Puebla. About ninety thousand Mexicans fluently speak Totonac dialects, with over one million of substantial Totonac ancestry.

CHICHIMECA

A reference to the Nahua peoples' term for outsiders—nomadic and semi-nomadic groups—in the Bajío region of Mexico. The term was later adopted by the Spanish with a pejorative connotation, and also refers to a language and a region known as La Gran Chichimeca.

ARTIST Fox Spears, *Blue Mountain Dream Journey*, Karuk

Map of Indigenous Nations

Please note: Although this map covers many Indigenous nations, there are still many more subgroups, regional identities, and uncontacted nations. The colors on the map correspond with the region name.

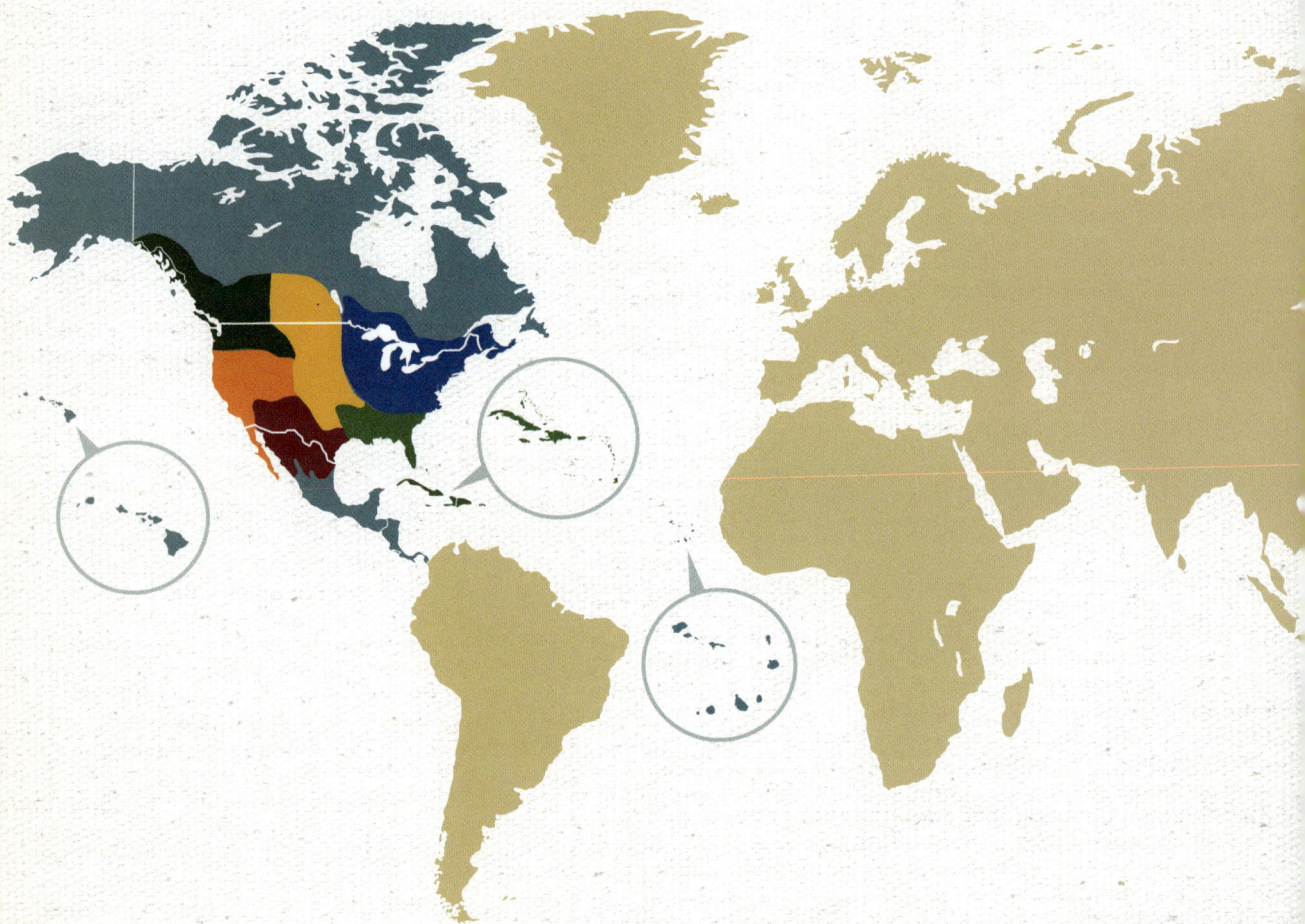

EASTERN WOODLANDS

Nations held territory within the upper Atlantic Coast of the United States and Canada and well into Central Time zones, including New York, Connecticut, Vermont, Maine, Rhode Island, Massachusetts, Michigan, and eastern Wisconsin.

Abenaki, Lenape, Mohawk, Mohegan, Mohican, Oneida, Passamaquoddy, Penobscot, Seaconke Wampanoag, Shinnecock, Stockbridge-Munsee

SOUTHEAST

These Nations controlled much of what are now considered the Southern United States and the Caribbean, including the Carolinas, Florida, and Cuba. Additionally, many of these nations were forcibly removed from their southern lands and pushed west into Indian Territory, today's Oklahoma.

Cherokee, Chickasaw, Haliwa-Saponi, Lipan Apache, Mvskoke (Creek), Nuyakv, Seminole, Taíno (Puerto Rico, Cuba, and Hispaniola)

GREAT PLAINS

Nations of this region roamed vast landscapes bordered by the Rocky Mountains in the West, the Mississippi and Missouri rivers in the East, and spanned North through the Dakotas into Canada and south past Colorado.

Apsáalooke (Crow), Arapaho, Arikara, Assiniboine, Blackfeet, Dakota, Ho-Chunk, Hidatsa, Ioway, Kickapoo, Kiowa, Lakota, Mandan, Northern Cheyenne, Odawa, Ojibwe, Omaha, Pawnee, Ziibiwing Anishinaabek (Saginaw Chippewa), Zaka'aaganing Anishinaabek (Sokaogon Ojibwe), Southern Cheyenne, Sioux

SOUTHWEST

Nations of this region continue to care for lands in today's Utah, Colorado, New Mexico, Arizona, Southern California, and Northern Mexico.

Akimel O'odham (Pima), Hopi, Laguna Pueblo, Navajo, Pascua Yaqui (Yoeme), Piipaash (Maricopa), Quechan, Tohono O'odham (Pima), Zuni (A:shiwi)

PACIFIC NORTHWEST

The territories of these Nations included areas up and down the entire Pacific Coastline of the United States and Canada, including Washington, Oregon, Northern California, Idaho, and British Columbia.

Cayuse, Clackamas, Grand Ronde, Lummi, Makah, Nimíipuu, Nisqually, Quinault, Santiam Kalapuya, Shasta, Siletz, S'Klallam, Spokane, Takelma, Tulalip, Umatilla, Watlala Chinook, Willamette Tumwater, Chinook, Yakama

CALIFORNIA

Hundreds of Nations protected the lands of this region, which also include east into Nevada, north into Oregon, and south into Mexico.

Acjachemen, Hupa, Karuk, Kumeyaay, Maidu (Mechoopda), Payómkawichum (Luiseño), Tongva, Yurok

BEYOND BORDERS

Indigeneity rejects colonial borders worldwide.

Alaska
Alutiiq, Chugach Alutiiq, Eyak, Iñupiat, Koyukon Athabascan, Neets'aii Gwich'in, Valdez

Hawai'i
Kānaka Maoli (Native Hawaiian)

Canada
Assiniboine, Blackfeet, Dene, Kitsumkalum, Métis, Nêhiyaw (Plains Cree), Nisga'a, N'laka'pamux, Ojibwe, Saulteaux, Ts'msyen/Tsimshian

Mexico
Kumeyaay, Mestiza, Pascua Yaqui (Yoeme), Tohono O'odham, Totonac

Africa
Cape Verdean (Cape Verde Islands)

Oceania
Samoan (Samoa and American Samoa)

Bibliography

EVERYDAY WARRIORS

U.S. House Committee on Commerce, Subcommittee on Oversight and Investigations. *The Olympics Site Selection Process: Remarks Before the Subcommittee on Oversight and Investigations*. 106th Cong., December 15, 1999. Testimony of Billy Mills, 1964 Olympic Gold Medalist. www.govinfo.gov/content/pkg/CHRG-106hhrg60363/html/CHRG-106hhrg60363.htm. Retrieved February 25, 2025.

Waters, Lindy. "Lindy Waters III Wasn't Surprised When Warriors Acquired Him." *NBC Sports Bay Area*, July 3, 2024. San Francisco, CA. https://www.nbcsportsbayarea.com/nba/golden-state-warriors/lindy-waters-iii-wasnt-surprised-when-warriors-acquired-him/1752161/.

STORIES AND TELLERS

U.S. House Appropriations Subcommittee on Interior, Environment, and Related Agencies. *2025 Appropriations Testimony for U.S. Fish and Wildlife Service, BIA/BIE, and HIS*. 118th Cong., May 7, 2024. Written testimony of Hon. W. Ron Allen, Tribal Chairman/CEO, Jamestown S'Klallam Tribe. docs.house.gov/meetings/AP/AP06/20240507/117269/HHRG-118-AP06-Wstate-AllenW-20240507.pdf. Retrieved February 23, 2025.

U.S. Senate Committee on Indian Affairs. *Oversight Hearing on the Impact of Racist Stereotypes on Indigenous People*. 112th Cong., May 6, 2011. Written testimony of Charlene Teters, Institute of American Indian Arts. www.govinfo.gov/content/pkg/CHRG-112shrg66994/pdf/CHRG-112shrg66994.pdf. Retrieved March 1, 2025.

U.S. House Select Committee on the Climate Crisis. *Tribal Voices, Tribal Wisdom: Strategies for the Climate Crisis*. 117th Cong., November 18, 2021. Written testimony of Fawn Sharp, President of the National Congress of American Indians, pp. 13–14.

ROOTS AND RELATIONS

U.S. Commission on Civil Rights. *Virtual Public Briefing: Assessing COVID-19 and the Broken Promises to Native Americans*. July 10, 2020. Written testimony of Lynn Malerba, Chief of the Mohegan Tribe and Secretary for the United South and Eastern Tribes Sovereignty Protection Fund Board of Directors. www.usccr.gov/files/2020/2020-07-17-Lynn-Malerba-Testimony.pdf. Retrieved February 22, 2025.

U.S. House Appropriations Subcommittee on Interior, Environment, and Related Agencies. *American Indian and Alaska Native Public Witness Day 2 Afternoon Session*. 116th Cong., February 12, 2020. Written testimony of Tehassi Tasi Hill, Oneida Nation Chairman. www.congress.gov/116/meeting/house/110493/witnesses/HHRG-116-AP06-Wstate-TasiHillT-20200212.pdf. Retrieved February 24, 2025.

U.S. House Committee on Natural Resources, Subcommittee on Indigenous Peoples of the United States. *Hybrid Legislative Hearing in Support of H.R. 5444, the Truth and Healing Commission on Indian Boarding School Policies Act of 2021*. 117th Cong., May 12, 2022. Written testimony of Kansas Representative Sharice L. Davids. www.congress.gov/117/meeting/house/114732/documents/HHRG-117-II24-MState-D000629-20220512.pdf. Retrieved February 28, 2025.

U.S. Senate Appropriations Committee. *Hearings of the Department of the Interior and Related Agencies.* 109th Cong., March 10, 2005. Written testimony of Charles Norman Shay. www.govinfo.gov/content/pkg/CHRG-109shrg99866/pdf/CHRG-109shrg99866.pdf. Retrieved March 2, 2025.

VanZile, Robert Jr. *Remarks to the U.S. Department of Education, White House Initiative on American Indian and Alaska Native Education, School Environment Listening Sessions Final Report.* 2015. Oral remarks, p. 19. files.eric.ed.gov/fulltext/ED614377.pdf. Retrieved February 24, 2025.

INNOVATORS AND INFLUENCERS

American Academy of Arts and Sciences. *Ms. Suzan Shown Harjo.* Accessed February 25, 2025. https://www.amacad.org/person/suzan-shown-harjo.

Studi, Wes. *Testimony for the Hearing "A Way Out of the Diabetes Crisis in Indian Country and Beyond."* Before the Senate Committee on Indian Affairs, 111th Congress, June 30, 2010. Accessed February 23, 2025. https://www.indian.senate.gov/wpcontent/uploads/upload/files/WesStudiTestimony.pdf.

U.S. Senate Committee on Indian Affairs. *Testimony for the Oversight Hearing on Economic Development.* 117th Cong., March 16, 2022. Written testimony of Janie Simms Hipp, General Counsel, U.S. Department of Agriculture. www.indian.senate.gov/wpcontent/uploads/3.16.2022%20Janie%20Simms%20Hipp_USDA_%20Testimony%20FINAL.pdf. Retrieved February 23, 2025.

U.S. Senate Committee on Indian Affairs. *Testimony for the Oversight Hearing "Stolen Identities: The Impact of Racist Stereotypes on Indigenous People"* 112th Cong., May 5, 2011. Written testimony of Suzan Shown Harjo, President, Morning Star Institute. www.indian.senate.gov/wp-content/uploads/Suzan%20Harjo%20testimony.pdf. Retrieved February 22, 2025.

U.S. House Committee on Natural Resources, Subcommittee on Indian and Insular Affairs. *Testimony Before the U.S. House of Representatives.* 118th Cong., March 24, 2023. Written testimony of Marcellus Osceola Jr., Tribal Council Chairman, Seminole Tribe of Florida. www.congress.gov/118/meeting/house/115538/witnesses/HHRG-118-II24-Wstate-OsceolaM-20230324.pdf. Retrieved February 25, 2025.

DESERT HEARTWORK

Bowekaty, Carleton. *Testimony for the Oversight Hearing "Examining the History of Federal Lands and the Development of Tribal Co-Management,"* Before the House Committee on Natural Resources, 117th Congress, March 8, 2022. Accessed February 24, 2025. https://www.govinfo.gov/content/pkg/CHRG-117hhrg47061/html/CHRG-117hhrg47061.htm.

Carlos, Mikah. *Testimony Regarding Tribal Child Welfare Services and the Title IV-B Program.* Field Hearing on Empowering Native American and Rural Communities, Before the House Ways and Means Committee, 118th Congress, May 10, 2024, Scottsdale, Arizona. Accessed February 28, 2025. https://waysandmeans.house.gov/wp-content/uploads/2024/05/Carlos-Testimony1.pdf.

Haaland, Deb. *Remarks on "Historic Progress in Indian Country."* White House Tribal Nations Summit, Washington, D.C., December 6, 2023. Accessed February 28, 2025. https://www.doi.gov/pressreleases/secretary-haaland-delivers-remarks-historic-progress-indian-country-during-2023-white/.

RECONNECTING THE SACRED

Risling Baldy, Cutcha. *"Give It Back: Publishing and Native Sovereignty."* Opening plenary, Association of University Presses Conference, delivered via Zoom, June 15, 2020. http://www.cutcharislingbaldy.com/blog/.

BEYOND BORDERS

Canada. Senate Standing Committee on Aboriginal Peoples. *Proceedings of the Standing Committee on Aboriginal Peoples.* 43rd Parliament, 2nd Session, February 17, 2021. Statement of Chief Mel Grandjamb, Fort McKay First Nation. https://sencanada.ca/en/Content/Sen/Committee/432/APPA/06ev-55242-e. Retrieved March 6, 2025.

Kastelic, Sarah. *Testimony from the First Hearing of the Advisory Committee of the Attorney General's Task Force on American Indian/Alaska Native Children Exposed to Violence.* U.S. Department of Justice, December 9, 2013. Accessed March 1, 2025. https://www.justice.gov/sites/default/files/defendingchildhood/legacy/2014/04/21/intersection-dv-cpsa.pdf.

Peter, Evon. *Testimony Before the Task Force on American Indian/Alaska Native Children Exposed to Violence.* Delivered in Anchorage, AK, June 12, 2014. Referenced in the U.S. Department of Justice report, *Attorney General's Advisory Committee on American Indian and Alaska Native Children Exposed to Violence: Ending Violence So Children Can Thrive,* November 2014, 130, 140. Accessed February 26, 2025.https://www.justice.gov/sites/default/files/defendingchildhood/pages/attachments/2014/11/18/finalaianreport.pdf.

Smith, William. *Testimony for the Briefing on COVID-19 in Indian Country: The Impact of Federal Broken Promises on Native Americans.* Before the U.S. Commission on Civil Rights, July 17, 2020. National Indian Health Board. Accessed February 28, 2025. https://www.usccr.gov/files/2020/2020-07-17-William-Smith-Testimony.pdf.

About the Author

TATÉ WALKER (THEY/THEM) is Mniconjou Lakota and a citizen of the Cheyenne River Sioux Tribe. They are an award-winning Two Spirit storyteller, and their illustrated poetry collection, *The Trickster Riots* (2022), earned Walker a 2022 Pushcart Prize nomination that same year. Additionally, Walker has written, photographed, and/or edited for various outlets, including *The Nation, Yellow Medicine Review, Studies in American Indian Literature, Apartment Therapy, Everyday Feminism, Native Peoples*, and *Indian Country Today*. They are also featured in several anthologies: *FIERCE: Essays by and about Dauntless Women* (2018), *South Dakota in Poems* (2019), *W.W. Norton's Everyone's an Author, 4e* (2020-2023), and *Good Eats: 32 Writers on Eating Ethically* (2024). Walker is a co-founder of the Phoenix Two Spirit Community group, which helps organize the annual Arizona Two Spirit Powwow and Rainbow Gathering. They are a longtime member of—and also serve on the board of directors for—the Oceti Sakowin Writers Society, which has a mission to mentor, empower, and promote Lakota, Dakota, and Nakota literary traditions. Walker is a 2023 ASU Poetry and the Senses Fellow and the 2023 Storyknife Fireweed Fellow. Walker has twenty years of experience in print/digital journalism and advocacy writing and is a trusted community builder within/for social justice and tribal education spaces. Learn more at www.jtatewalker.com.

About the Artists

Jordan Ann Craig

Stop Flirting With Me (back cover),
Nothing is Enough for You (p. 12)

Art photography by Tonee Harbert.

Confessions of a Fairy Goddess
(p. 30-31)

Courtesy the artist and Hales, London and New York. Art photography by James Hart Photography.

See profile on page 30.

Steve Smith (Dla'kwagila)

Eagle Chilkat (p. 2), *Eagle's Essence* (p. 40)

Steve Smith (Dla'kwagila) has been carving and painting since 1987. Initially taught by his father, Harris Smith, in the Oweekeno and Kwakwaka'wakw style, Steve has since developed his own distinct and innovative style. Steve's pieces include original paintings, sculptures, masks, limited edition prints, etched glass, totem poles, and drums. His cutting edge work has been featured in several major exhibitions throughout North America, and has been purchased by collectors around the world. Steve resides in Vancouver, BC, Canada with his wife and daughter.

Lehuauakea

Kānehunamoku (p. 4-5),
Mana Māhū (p. 144)

Lehuauakea is a Native Hawaiian interdisciplinary artist and cultural practitioner from Pāpaʻikou, Hawaiʻi. With a particular focus on the making of kapa (barkcloth), ʻohe kāpala (carved bamboo printing tools), and use of natural pigments, Lehua breathes new life into patterns and traditions practiced for generations. Through these traditional Native Hawaiian customs and gathered organic materials, their work addresses themes related to environmental stewardship, an evolving contemporary Hawaiian identity, and the teachings held in cultural mythologies and cosmologies. Lehuauakea is currently based between the continent and Pāpaʻikou after earning their Bachelor of Fine Arts in Painting Pacific Northwest College of Art.

Elias Jade Not Afraid

Geometric Florals (p. 18-19)

See profile on page 18.

Hattie Lee Mendoza

Having Company (p. 6), *Majesty* (p. 88)

Hattie Lee Mendoza is a multi-disciplinary artist who grew up in Fowler, Kansas, and now lives in Peoria, Illinois.

A member of the Cherokee Nation, Hattie's process is a personal expression of the Native American diaspora. Being herself a collage of cultures, Hattie creates by collaging materials from her ancestors, contemporary community, and personal experiences.

Hattie's studio is a flux of mediums and objects in constant conversation: Nothing is off-limits to being repurposed and reimagined. Graphic design, fine art, and craft are woven together there, and cultivating the joy that arises from cultural differences gives hope for future tribes, countries, and personal communities.

Jessica Leigh Gokey

Woodland Floral (front cover), *Diana* (p. 66)

Jessica Leigh Gokey is a bead artist from the Lac Courte Oreilles Band of Lake Superior Ojibwe near Hayward, Wisconsin. She lives in Trego, Wisconsin, with her family and has been beading for over 15 years. Inspired as a child by watching her aunt bead—a tradition passed down by an elder—Jessica has honed her skills with the guidance of fellow artists and knowledge-keepers.

She specializes in traditional Ojibwe floral designs, using her beadwork as a way to keep cultural traditions alive. Jessica is passionate about sharing her knowledge with others and regularly teaches beadwork in both local and distant communities. Her fine art beadwork is held in museum collections in Minnesota and Michigan, and she has been commissioned to create custom pieces for collectors across the region.

Debra Yepa-Pappan

Corn Maiden (Leads the Way) (p. 108)

Debra Yepa-Pappan (Jemez Pueblo and Korean) is a visual artist and the co-founding director of exhibitions and programs at the Center for Native Futures, a vibrant contemporary art space located in Downtown Chicago that is dedicated to supporting Native artists. Her multimedia art practice combines digital collage and photography, focusing on themes related to her mixed-race identity, cultural heritage, family, and home, incorporating Pueblo and urban aesthetics. Her works can be found in various museum and private collections worldwide. Debra lives in Chicago, Illinois with her husband, artist Chris Pappan, and their daughter, performing artist Ji Hae Yepa-Pappan.

Fox Spears

Running Ridge (endpapers),
Verdant Mountain (p. 128),
Blue Mountain Dream Journey (p. 183)

Fox Spears is a contemporary visual artist working across multiple mediums that include monotype printmaking, drawing, painting, and 3D objects. He is an enrolled member of the Karuk Tribe and frequently looks to traditional Karuk culture as inspiration for the art he creates. Born and raised in the Pacific Northwest, he was a lifelong resident of the greater Seattle, Washington area until 2022. He currently resides with his husband in Orlando, Florida.

First published in 2025 by Wellfleet Press,
an imprint of The Quarto Group,
142 West 36th Street, 4th Floor,
New York, NY 10018, USA
(212) 779-4972 www.Quarto.com

EEA Representation, WTS Tax d.o.o.,
Žanova ulica 3, 4000 Kranj, Slovenia.
www.wts-tax.si

Wellfleet titles are also available at discount
for retail, wholesale, promotional, and bulk
purchase. For details, contact the Special Sales
Manager by email at specialsales@quarto.com
or by mail at The Quarto Group, Attn: Special
Sales Manager, 100 Cummings Center Suite
265D, Beverly, MA 01915 USA.

10 9 8 7 6 5 4 3 2 1

ISBN: 978-1-57715-491-4

Digital edition published in 2025
eISBN: 978-0-7603-9370-3

Library of Congress Control Number:
2025933910

Group Publisher: Rage Kindelsperger
Editorial Director: Erin Canning
Creative Director: Laura Drew
Senior Art Director: Marisa Kwek
Cover Design: Marisa Kwek
Interior Design: Tara Long
Managing Editor: Cara Donaldson
Editor: Keyla Pizarro-Hernández
Front Cover: Jessica Leigh Gokey
Back Cover: Jordan Ann Craig
Endpapers: Fox Spears

Printed in Huizhou, Guangdong, China
TT082025

This book provides general information on
various widely known and widely accepted
images that tend to evoke feelings of strength
and confidence. However, it should not be
relied upon as recommending or promoting any
specific diagnosis or method of treatment for a
particular condition, and it is not intended as a
substitute for medical or mental health advice or
for direct diagnosis and treatment of a medical or
mental health condition by a qualified physician.
Readers who have questions about a particular
condition, possible treatments for that condition,
or possible reactions from the condition or its
treatment should consult a physician or other
qualified healthcare professional.

The Quarto Group denounces any and all forms
of hate, discrimination, and oppression and
does not condone the use of its products in any
practices aimed at harming or demeaning any
group or individual.